NATURAL
CURIOSITY

of related interest

Learning without School
Home Education
Ross Mountney
ISBN 978 1 84310 685 2
eISBN 978 1 84642 863 0

Choosing Home
Deciding to Homeschool with Asperger's Syndrome
Martha Kennedy Hartnett and Stephen M. Shore
ISBN 978 1 84310 763 7
eISBN 978 1 84642 171 6

Home Educating Our Autistic Spectrum Children
Paths are Made by Walking
Edited by Terri Dowty and Kitt Cowlishaw
ISBN 978 1 84310 037 9
eISBN 978 1 84642 190 7

NATURAL CURIOSITY

Educating and Nurturing Our Children at Home

Lisa Carne

Foreword by Dr Alan Thomas

Jessica Kingsley *Publishers*
London and Philadelphia

Quote on page 170 is reproduced from *India of My Dreams* (2008) with kind permission from Rajpal & Sons, Kashmere Gate, Delhi.

First published in 2016
by Jessica Kingsley Publishers
73 Collier Street
London N1 9BE, UK
and
400 Market Street, Suite 400
Philadelphia, PA 19106, USA

www.jkp.com

Library of Congress Cataloging in Publication Data
Names: Carne, Lisa, 1969-
Title: Natural curiosity : educating and nurturing our children at home / Lisa Carne ; foreword by Dr. Alan Thomas.
Description: London : Jessica Kingsley Publishers, 2016.
Identifiers: LCCN 2015048794 | ISBN 9781785920332 (alkaline paper)
Subjects: LCSH: Carne, Lisa, 1969- | Carne, Lisa, 1969---Family. | Home schooling--United States. | Home schooling--Philosophy. | Natural history--Study and teachiing--United States. | Environmental education--United States. | Education--Parent participation--United States.
Classification: LCC LC40 .C373 2016 | DDC 371.04/2--dc23 LC record available at http://lccn.loc.gov/2015048794

British Library Cataloguing in Publication Data
A CIP catalogue record for this book is available from the British Library

ISBN 978 1 78592 033 2
eISBN 978 1 78450 288 1

Printed and bound in Great Britain

*For the three wonders of my world
and Little Lord Douglas,
a loyal companion*

Young naturalists are an endangered species,
mainly due to habitat restriction,
but they are not yet extinct...
There is a way to increase numbers and make a difference

CONTENTS

FOREWORD

Lisa Carne's starting point in this original and fascinating book is that today, more than ever, we need to be more aware of and knowledgeable about the natural world, and that we have to be part of it, not to dominate and exploit it. Perhaps the best resource we have, she argues, is children, who are naturally and often insatiably curious about the world around them, its flora and fauna.

During my research into home education I have often found myself going out for walks with families. I can recall many occasions when the children have been astounded by my lack of knowledge of the natural world. On a walk in the Norfolk Fens with one family, the eleven-year-old could hardly believe that I did not recognize a pheasant or that I had never heard of a great crested grebe, which he was excited to spot. Even my home-educated six-year-old grandson knows more about the natural world than I do, partly inspired by his parents' interest.

We often hear about teachers who criticize the current situation in school, especially primary school, and being forced to follow an arid curriculum. It's not that different from my own primary education in the 1940s. One common complaint is that there is no time to foster a love of the natural world. Lisa Carne has not only introduced her two home-educated children to the natural world; she has gone much further and demonstrated how an enthusiasm for all things natural can encompass a full educational curriculum.

The common picture of the home educating family is that of parent and child sitting at the kitchen table and following a set curriculum, not unlike what would be experienced in school. While some parents might follow this route, certainly when they start out, they usually find that school methods do not really serve their children well and find themselves pioneering new educational approaches. In particular they are able to follow their children's interests, simply acting as guide or mentor, certainly until the need for formal qualifications arises.

Home education has always been legal, though until relatively recently the practice was viewed askance by the authorities and anything that deviated from school methods would not have been tolerated. Over the last twenty years or so numbers have grown rapidly and there are now possibly 80,000 home-educated children in the UK. In consequence they have a voice to influence the authorities, and current government guidelines acknowledge that parents are free to follow their own philosophy. This allows them to adapt to their children's interests and styles of learning. Lisa points out that her daughter is an 'avid writer', while her son is more 'hands on', and that she encourages both approaches.

Lisa demonstrates how her two children are being educated through their fascination with the world around them. As she says, all the basics are to be found in nature: science, literature, art, maths and literacy. One might add just about everything else worth knowing. There is always something to arouse and extend a child's interest. For example, when one of the children asked 'Why do we blink?' they found that geckos have no eyelids so they lick their eyes to clean and moisten them.

It's not that Lisa pushes the natural world at her children – she may have drawn their attention to it from the start but it's just as likely to be the case that they take off in their own right. It's not narrow either; as she says, 'All that a child finds interesting should be seen as relevant to their learning.'

The children constantly ask questions which not only increase their knowledge but also lead to acquiring research know-how. Interestingly, I recall talking to a girl who started school for the first time when she was eleven. She couldn't understand why the teacher was asking all the questions when it was the children who were doing all the learning! Here are just a few questions that Lisa's children have raised: Can shadows be in colour? Is the moon moving? What's a rip current? Why are people vegetarian? When is the next eclipse? What's a ceasefire baby? What is magnetism?

Most of all, Lisa's engaging book, full of observations and reflections, shows up the wonders of the natural world and is not just relevant to home educators but also to schools, especially in describing how we should all live in wonder at how the natural world has evolved and how we should look after it. In doing so she has not only written a fascinating and very readable account but also contributed a realistic and original alternative to mainstream education. As she points out, its message is not confined to home education; all parents can introduce a love of nature to their children and help ensure that future generations will take care of the planet.

Dr Alan Thomas
Developmental psychologist and
co-author of How Children Learn at Home

ACKNOWLEDGEMENTS

This book has a journey of discovery behind it, leading directly to its existence, and it would not have evolved without the curiosity, kindness and patience of others. Therefore I would like to thank all the 'others' who have helped to bring this book to life. Firstly, my two wonderful children for placing their trust in me and for being true to themselves. Then my fabulous husband, Ian, for his unwavering support and for sharing the helm...the journey continues. If I hadn't enjoyed such a happy childhood I probably wouldn't be writing today and so I would like to take this opportunity to thank my late father, for being the true family man that he was, and my mother for being the kind matriarch that she is. I would like to thank and express my sincere gratitude to Dr Alan Thomas for his interest and of course his Foreword. And finally, my grateful thanks to Hannah Shakespeare, Emily Gowers, Alexandra Holmes and the team at Jessica Kingsley Publishers for making the publication process such a pleasure.

INTRODUCTION

This book has been written out of respect for children and as a gentle reminder that as one of nature's species we are unable to disconnect from nature. Thus, it is perhaps recognition of this and not reconnection with nature that is needed when we look to establish a child's bond with their natural world.

My own children (and all children) have a natural fascination with the world that sustains them; this may seem obvious for a species that relies on their environment for survival. Many parents naturally trust their instincts when it comes to nurturing their children and some will recognize the importance of developing an infant's fascination with their natural environment.

Most parents are also particularly good at ensuring that kindness finds its way into their children's lives, and my own parents provided kindness in abundance. As a result, my sister and I spent many of our childhood days being happy at home with our mother, who ensured we had time to play, took the time to read to us and would often make up adventure stories of her own. In short, she nurtured us. Equally I enjoyed spending time with my father and in return he had a great deal of time and respect for us as children. We spent considerable lengths of time outdoors where we would play alongside him as he worked in the garden. So you could say we had a content childhood: a family at home enjoying each other's company. And then along came school.

My sister went first, quite happily as my mother recalls, but her enthusiasm was short lived. She thought she only had to go for one day and so she wasn't particularly pleased when she found herself having to go again the next day. Two years later it was my turn and I didn't understand why I had to go either; my parents remained patient and encouraged me daily but I just didn't think school was the right place for me to be.

I persevered in the school environment and I can remember my last year in junior (primary) school; we didn't have the same 'push' for results that children face today, but I do recall we had a class teacher who was a little unforgiving in her approach, particularly when it came to literature. This teacher was a joy to be in the company of outdoors when tending the school garden but when she was teaching in the classroom she became pretty miserable to say the least. One afternoon she bellowed at me, 'How dare you look out of the window when I'm talking to you?' She was so angry her hair shook when she spoke, but dare I did, daily, with sad frustrated sighs. I remember this teacher being absolutely adamant that she would never read the work of Enid Blyton to us in her classroom and I found this very odd; after all, she had asked the class for suggestions and Enid Blyton had been my choice as these were books I was enjoying at home. My mother would often read them to me and this remains a treasured memory from my childhood.

My husband and I are often reminded of moments like these when we compare our own experiences of school. Disruptive and badly behaved pupils plagued our secondary schools, and in my teenage years I would occasionally escape from school with my friend. Yes...we played truant (my husband, on the other hand, did not). This was considered bad behaviour by teaching professionals and so we were deemed to be brave amongst some pupils and no doubt foolish in the eyes of others; either way we managed to remain popular with our peers. The simple fact was that we wanted to talk to each other and would encourage ourselves to dart hastily out of the little school gate straight into the beautiful public gardens that were rather temptingly just opposite our school grounds. There we could choose whether to sit in the sun or shade, under the tree or by the pond; any of these would naturally be preferable to being confined in a disruptive classroom setting.

Sadly, little appears to have changed over the years as unruly behaviour and class disruption continue to plague many of our schools today.

Eventually my own school days came to an end and full-time employment followed. Ten years or so after leaving school, in 1994, I met a handsome (albeit unemployed) photographer who had returned to the area after living and working at the foot of the Malvern Hills in Worcestershire. He soon became employed and we purchased our first home, a five-hundred-year-old one-bedroomed cottage. We enjoyed our early years of married life in this ivy-clad cottage but space was extremely limited and so we moved to our first family-sized home. It was here in 2003 that we became parents for the first time (a son) and then again in 2005 (a daughter).

We immediately found ourselves placing trust in our own parenting instincts and without even realizing it at the time we were nurturing through nature. Our children established an early bond with each other and with nature and it appeared that because of these bonds they matured quickly in their early years. Looking back now, we remember them as being particularly content, alert and happy babies. We moved again twice in their early years before settling into our current home.

As young children in their new rural home with its large and wild garden (secret almost, as the house and gardens are hidden behind gates), they had the environment and security needed to play and develop their bonds further, and we nurtured them while ensuring they had kindness in their lives. I read many books to them, including Enid Blyton, and I made up stories of my own. As a family we would often take a detour on our journey home to see our very first home and these days there's a chorus of 'there it is' when the little ivy-clad cottage comes into view. At the weekends they would spend time out in the garden with their father and on weekdays they would enjoy spending time together, just the two of them, often outdoors and with me nearby watching out for them. They had the wonders of the natural world to explore in an environment where they could listen, observe, touch, sit, sleep and above all play freely. They were natural observers of nature, developing a bond with it as they grew and were driven to ask many questions. This naturally led them to **E**xplore, **P**onder, **I**magine and **C**reate: their EPIC education as it was to become known to them.

All family members relied on their own instincts, and as a result strong bonds with nature soon became established through this natural nurturing style. Our children's learning journey at home became fascinating to observe as I began to research when and how children establish close bonds with nature. We were learning side by side, each of us fuelling the others' interests and at our own pace. As a family it enriched us, and our own knowledge and understanding of the natural world grew when we were mindful of our children's curiosity.

Having already settled into their home learning environment my children weren't expecting to go to school, but unlike my sister and I they were given a choice. They both knew they didn't have to go to pre-school to play or school to learn; they could carry on playing and learning at home if they preferred. This gave them the opportunity from a very young age to naturally follow any path of interest that would feed their instinctive curiosity and to choose where they preferred to learn.

Having tried and enjoyed playing at their local pre-school, they both chose to go to school and they did in fact stay in their school environments longer than I anticipated. They were, however, extremely determined to remain loyal to the natural world and would persistently incorporate elements from it into their play with friends and also in their classroom work. Towards the end of their primary school years they found that incorporating their valued interests into their school environment was becoming extremely difficult. An increase in the pressure placed upon them and the continuous push to succeed meant they developed an overwhelming sense that the path ahead would lead them away from learning through their interest in the natural world and into a testing environment where mathematics would become everybody's top priority and focus. My son was the first to discover how this persistent pressure could cast a shadow over the joy of learning through natural curiosity.

A time of deliberation followed and in 2014 our eleven-year-old son and his nine-year-old sister decided to opt out of their schools. They placed trust in their own ability to learn through the natural habit of being curious and by pursuing their own established paths of interest. They continue to gain valuable knowledge this way in the only environment that enables them to have uninhibited access to the natural world daily...their home.

The important thing is not to stop questioning.
Curiosity has its own reason for existing.

Albert Einstein (1955)

Chapter One

NURTURE THROUGH NATURE

Many ask if it is nature or nurture that defines a child; I think it's this –

Nature (N) + Nurture (Nt) + Natural World (Nw) = Child (C)

$$C = N + Nt + Nw$$

The good news is you don't have to be a scientist, mathematician or naturalist to figure out this equation, as nurturing a child's bond to nature is a simple and natural process. You will soon be surprised at the life-enhancing benefits it can have for you and your family. We are not alone in doing this, of course; many mammals nurture their young in this way as it is essential for the survival of a species.

This book is essentially about being a human parent as we discover that it is not in the best interest of our infants to turn their attention away from what naturally sustains them; in doing so we could unwittingly be sealing the fate of future generations and even the survival of our own species.

Having been fascinated by the chemistry of how infants develop a bond with nature, my research led me to the work of greater minds than mine:

For much of human evolution, the natural world constituted one of the most important contexts children encountered during their critical years of maturation. It would not be too bold to assert that direct and indirect experience of nature has been and may possibly remain a critical component

21

in human physical, emotional, intellectual and even moral development. (Kahn and Kellert 2002, p.vii)

After eleven years of observing this in my own children by nurturing through nature from infancy, I am of the opinion that both parent and child can gain valuable knowledge through this process.

EXAMPLE: If a bird is seen in the garden gathering nest material (and I don't have to know what type of bird it is) I will softly call out to my children and point it out. If they are interested in having a look (and they naturally are) they join me and we quietly wait in the hope of locating the nest site. This triggers many questions; for instance, they may wonder about the bird's choice of material for its nest. When they were younger they were more inclined to follow my suggestions and rush off to try to find out what type of bird it was; being particularly keen to share their knowledge they would quickly return with their thoughts or findings. Other times I would join them and help with the identification and I soon discovered that my own knowledge was being enhanced in the process of educating my children.

What became apparent is how naturally they brought nature into their lives daily. As they grew their continued casual interest in birds led them to become aware of when certain birds would appear in the garden or when they would leave to migrate. This introduced them to the seasons, climate, oceans, distance and an awareness of other countries; their knowledge soon surpassed mine. I'm pretty good at finding oceans and countries on a world map but my children now have a tendency to find them first!

I knew they were not only learning but also retaining knowledge just by what they were relaying back to me during conversations, and they would incorporate this knowledge into their play daily.

EXAMPLE: When my son was younger and needed help to trim his fingernails it would often be a reminder for him to share the fact that our nails were made out of the same substance that a rhino's horn is made of. On each occasion he would repeat the fact in the same way and this would be a trigger for us both to look again at our nails and talk about them further. I would often ask him if he could remember what the substance was called and we would remind ourselves: keratin.

By being mindful and observing nature daily in their nurturing I have come to understand that there is a natural balance of respect that occurs between a parent, a child and the natural world when it comes to learning. A child asks questions or points out something of interest and a parent responds. In return the parent searches for items of interest to introduce to the child. I do this by focusing on the natural world, as I have always instinctively felt that it shouldn't be left out of the nurturing equation. As a family we simply enjoy observing and trying to understand what we see happening in the natural world and include it in our daily conversations; this includes questioning the more unusual as well as the obvious. A young child will soon develop an awareness that the smallest of species in nature is as extraordinary as the largest.

We are born ready to be nurtured and introduced to our natural environment. From the moment of birth we instinctively know how to get attention: we cry and expect a response and we develop facial expressions that can be read by our parents.

What is also clear to me is that we can nurture a habit to be mindful of the natural world, and this develops in both parent and child through the nurturing process.

My own children have grown up knowing that the curiosities of the natural world can be shared, and they will call for me or their father if they see something that interests them, be it outside, on their laptops, in a book or magazine or on the television. Being mindful self-fuels their interest, especially as they can now also view the natural world via technology. Any one of us can trigger a discussion as we discover and share what we read, see or think about, and as a family we continue to gain knowledge this way.

DISTRACTION: My children have just counted the number of starlings that are currently in the garden; they make quite a racket (the starlings, not the children). There are over a dozen.

I have referred to being 'mindful' of nature in this chapter and this is important. In today's modern world we are becoming increasingly aware of the importance of easing stress, and mindfulness is one way to achieve this. When children learn at home they are naturally mindful and focus on the moment; it's the adults around them who sometimes need reminding, myself included.

The modern world of parenting is a busy environment and there are so many demands and distractions that are difficult to ignore. What I can comfortably say is that I'm mindful of my children. I'm mindful of them and their needs, and that's essential. You can only nurture through nature if you take the time to establish a habit of observing it and show your children how important it is to protect and respect it. I will always endeavour to stop what I'm doing if I spot a nature distraction in order to point it out to the children.

To enable young children to develop a natural respect for nature we may need to show consideration when purchasing items such as wasp killer and ant powder, for instance. It's in the interest of our children that we should maintain our own curiosity for nature even if there are times when we feel bothered by it.

With a nature-fed education at home and no sign of natural history being introduced to their school curriculum, it was really no surprise that my own children felt confident enough to walk away from their schools in 2014 with a great sense of relief.

I took much pleasure in watching the habits of birds, and even made notes on the subject. In my simplicity, I remember wondering why every gentleman did not become an ornithologist.

Charles Darwin (1887)

Chapter Two

BORN FREE

I'd like to concentrate in this chapter on the importance of parents recognizing the balance of nurture through nature, as a parent's positive response to their child's interest will boost learning. Once a bond with nature has been established, a child will develop this further as they continue to remain curious and explore, ponder, imagine and create all the way through their early years and beyond. Through this, a young child will recognize how important it is to understand the world in which they live.

To encourage interest in nature further a diligent parent can enhance their child's knowledge by responding in a positive manner to all that a child finds fascinating, whether it be the tiniest spider or the largest! This is particularly important as a child is looking for a reaction to these new discoveries and will turn to their parent/role model for knowledge or reassurance, but with so much to do and see they won't ask twice if they can see for themselves that nature has no relevance to their parent or role model. So you may have to be brave and give that spider a helping hand out of your bathtub. I did, and our nine-year-old daughter still goes out of her way to save spiders and 'the little bug guys'; she even has her own cuddly spider called Dave who sits proudly in her soft toy collection. She could persuade you that jumping spiders are especially cute close up.

We already know that it's in a child's best interest to play outside and enjoy nature so they can appreciate and respect their environment. They should be given the time and freedom they need to explore their surroundings naturally, either alone or in the company of siblings but always under the watchful eye of an understanding parent or role model.

If you watch other young mammals in their natural environments you will see playful behaviour, for which they are often reprimanded by their parents if they push the boundaries. These mammals play freely for a reason and their parents keep them in line for the same reason. Together they establish the balanced behaviour needed in order to survive in their environment.

We can learn from these actions and the behaviour of other species. Elephants have caught my attention in recent years, as they appear to be a species that naturally respects the value of each family member. Each individual brings something to the group as they carry out the roles that nature intended in order for their species to survive. I have been learning a little more about this through the published work of Michael Garstang, a distinguished Emeritus Research Professor in Environmental Sciences at the University of Virginia.

> Much of elephant learning must be through observing group members, with individuals spending an entire lifetime within a single group continuously following older more knowledgeable relatives. The nearly two years that a calf nurses followed by eight to ten years of close contact with the mother and attention paid by allomothers to the calf provide an extended period of learning at a critical time of development for the calf. Almost uniquely among mammals, female elephants remain within a closely knit family unit for the rest of their lives. (Garstang 2015, p.91)

Elephants are exceptional mothers as they simply put to use the knowledge and wisdom gained from older generations. They appear to know rather than assume (as humans sometimes do) that the needs of their young are being met. We have this same responsibility to nurture just as other intelligent mammals do. But I think as parents, teachers and role models we may need to look again; perhaps look a little deeper into our own human instincts in the hope of providing living and learning environments that ensure all children experience respect and nurturing.

We do also have the responsibility (as parents) to ensure our children receive an education and I believe this should include an understanding of the natural world. Children can miss out on developing a bond with the natural world or acknowledging its benefits if they are not part of it. If they spend their days in a controlled environment they may find they have little time to explore their surroundings and play at will. Parents also miss out on the opportunity to pass on their wisdom at appropriate moments as they watch over them. We are mammals after all, a fact often overlooked by fashion trends and pressures applied by society and schools.

Wherever children prefer to be educated we can look to ensure that some casual references to nature find their way into their daily lives. Finding out the science behind animal behaviour is just one obvious example – how do domestic dogs compare to wild wolves? We talk with our children about such things and we enjoy finding out.

DISTRACTION: My children have 'dropped' a man into Australia on Google Maps. He's on the coast in New South Wales; they're trying to locate the home of their great aunt. This is a good example of how their curiosity (that strong urge to know or understand something) drove them to self-directed learning and in this particular instance led them to exploring New South Wales online.

Nurturing a child under the wing of the natural world is something that all role models could come to recognize. Offering singular isolated nature experiences is not enough to keep a child's curiosity about nature alive. I believe a more subtle daily approach is required. To offer nature as a holiday experience could appear to be just another recreational activity and deep down I think we all know the natural world means much more to us than that. We depend on it and yet we don't always show nature our respect. Jetting off to Africa to have a safari or sitting around a campfire toasting marshmallows (as lovely as this is) isn't what being nurtured through nature means. My children's curiosity changed my own perception and understanding as we discovered together that all nature (including the fascinating growth and spread of mould, for example) could be educational and interesting. Things that weren't an obvious consideration and/or aesthetically pleasing could still be of interest. I became aware of the importance of children working out why things happen in nature and understanding the purpose of any particular species. All role models could experience the benefits of daily nature observation with children, and this would shine through in the facial expressions of well-nurtured children and would last longer than the jet lag from any holiday.

 NOTE: I'm not suggesting holidays aren't educational: far from it, as most of us would enjoy an opportunity to learn about wildlife in other environments, cultures and countries. It's just that I wouldn't encourage children to form the impression that there are more exciting species to observe in other parts of the world as this may turn their attention away from developing an understanding of the fascinating wildlife living right under their noses.

Many naturalists, environmentalists and conservationists are of course already aware of the benefits gained from observing, respecting and protecting nature, and we can learn from their knowledge and discoveries from the comfort of our own home. As a family we continue to research their efforts via books and the Internet, taking a keen interest in their work.

The late South African conservationist Lawrence Anthony has shown through his fascinating work how important it is to acknowledge and think about how we treat other species. This is just one example of his many words of wisdom:

In our noisy cities we tend to forget the things our ancestors knew on a gut level: that the wilderness is alive, that its whispers are there for all to hear – and to respond to.

We also have to understand that there are things we cannot understand. Elephants possess qualities and abilities well beyond the means of science to decipher. Elephants cannot repair a computer, but they do have communication, physical and metaphysical, that would make Bill Gates's mouth drop open. In some very important ways they are ahead of us.

Some unexplained occurrences are quite evident throughout the plant and animal kingdom and there is nothing like looking at what is actually going on around you to turn a lot of what you always thought to be true on its head. (Anthony and Spence 2010, p.2)

We couldn't help but be moved when the elephants that he had developed a strong bond with on his Thula Thula game reserve in Zululand appeared to mourn his passing in 2012.

My own children have experienced for themselves how a mainstream education can underestimate their interest and role in the natural world, and it was up to me as their parent to recognize this. All parents need to be aware of the educational benefits an early bond to nature can have long before they have their attention turned away by technology and any target-driven school curriculum.

It was through my son's interest in the iguanas that inhabit the Galapagos Islands that I discovered more about the life of Charles Darwin and that of his grandfather, Erasmus Darwin. I remember thinking at the time that Mr Darwin (the younger) was maybe a little insensitive when he studied the behaviour of his own children, researching them in their natural environment; I thought that perhaps he saw them as a scientific curiosity.

I was wrong to think this as I can now see that all parents instinctively observe their own children and this is something we do naturally. I'm not an academic like Charles Darwin, but the interest has always been there for me. I have unknowingly been studying my children and learning with them; as a result I have seen for myself the relevance of Darwin's work and understand why he was so fascinated by his own children's behaviour.

NOTE: My own fascination has led me to understand why it is so important that we allow children to communicate their thoughts and play freely. I believe these are vital components to their development, education and general well being.

My first child was born on December 27th, 1839, and I at once commenced to make notes on the first dawn of the various expressions which he exhibited, for I felt convinced, even at this early period, that the most complex and fine shades of expression must all have had a gradual and natural origin.

Charles Darwin (1887)

Chapter Three

SO WHY AREN'T THEY IN SCHOOL?

When my children first started mainstream school I was able to observe their response to having to start learning again in a different way. This time they were going to be taught in groups where they would no longer have the time to follow their curiosity as the school would now decide what they should learn and when. In the case of both children their confusion and frustration were sometimes obvious to me but their polite manner and natural keenness to please eventually helped them to conform in the classroom. They soon made friends and for them this became a good reason to stay.

It was clear to them that their natural freedom to ask questions and follow their interests was no longer possible, but worst of all, they soon discovered they had limited time to play freely. So they knuckled down in organized groups to listen and learn, and were taught what the mainstream school system considered necessary for them to function, compete and live in a modern society. They soon found out that their outdoor interests hadn't been considered at all, and became accustomed to being tested regularly to ensure they were on target to reach the required standard. So school didn't hold much appeal, but their friendships were strong and so they stayed.

With the dismissal of their natural learning I wondered how it must feel to a child when their own early thoughts, opinions and interests take a back seat as they focus on what the teacher has to say instead. We naturally like to communicate and yet time and time again we hear children being silenced in a school environment as we continue to underestimate them; how many of us as adults could sit silent for that length of time, being chosen only occasionally to answer a question or contribute? We all instinctively like to join in and so would feel just as frustrated as some of the children do.

Over time they adjusted to school but their deflated state at being kept indoors to learn rather than playing and learning outdoors led us to reconsider home education. Children can have a pretty good idea of what they would like to play or think about daily; having already established an EPIC education (explore, ponder, imagine, create) at home I knew that my children were very capable of developing the skills they needed to pursue their early interests further in the safe and secure environment of their home.

DISTRACTION: My train of thought is being momentarily distracted by a familiar little voice. I'm now glancing across at my nine-year-old daughter as she asks, 'Why do we blink?' I smile and ask her politely, 'Why do you think we blink?' turning my laptop screen towards her, having quickly prepared the Google search screen ready to research online. Her eleven-year-old brother is looking at me now with wide eyes. 'It's to keep our eyes clean, isn't it?'

I answer 'Yes', although we now feel the need to research and check. 'Yep, look' I say... 'We blink to keep our eyeballs moist and clean.' I carry on scrolling down and reading out loud to them. 'Do you know hamsters blink with one eye at a time?' Naturally we all take the time to look at each other as we digest this information; all blinking, one eye at a time, as we look around. We discuss what hamsters might see, why their eyes are positioned that way and how this can help protect them from predators, and it's not long before the eyesight and hunting habits of other species are being discussed.

> **NOTE:** Geckos don't have eyelids and so they have to lick their eyeballs... Interestingly, we didn't even attempt to try this.

Having spent eleven years self-educating myself and learning alongside my children, first nurturing them through nature as infants and young children and then assisting them with their EPIC education and natural history interests, I can now look back and reflect on how their full and rich education has benefited all family members.

This style of teaching is not widely recognized in many schools, but we are aware of communities across the world that benefit from being mindful of nature. So there may be hope for all cultures and future generations as more of us become aware of this.

One leading environmentalist, HRH The Prince of Wales, saw for himself how effective this style of integrated teaching can be as he observed a project/workshop in a school environment. This is detailed in the fascinating book *Harmony*, which gives a brief insight into how the pupils and their teacher worked together to gain valuable knowledge. The lesson was geometry but the children didn't know this, as learning became the natural outcome through the study of patterns in nature.

> I have seen the children's feedback to the project and many of them say much the same thing, that nobody has ever told them before that such things as mathematics and science could be so joyful and revealing. They learn what they would learn in a conventional geometry lesson, but within a symbolic context, so they relate the knowledge that they gain to their own personal experience and, crucially, they remember it.
>
> I gather that the effect is quite infectious. Not only the children, but also their teachers who help during the workshops, say that by mid-week they cannot stop counting things.
>
> They have begun to see that there are very special, universal patterns everywhere in Nature that are just as apparent in their own bodies, and it is not long before they

begin to question what these mean to them and what such patterns say about their personal relationship with Nature. (HRH The Prince of Wales, Juniper and Skelly 2010, pp.278–9)

I can still remember the first time I came across this particular piece in the book. It was when we were together on a family holiday in Cornwall and this bit of the book gave me goose bumps! It was the moment that added extra clout to my many thoughts as I instantly saw the similarities with how my own children were acknowledging nature while being nurtured and educated at home.

This meant that what we had been doing at home could perhaps one day be introduced into mainstream schools. If parents could incorporate nurture through nature into their daily routines then this could potentially be carried on and encouraged throughout their children's schooling via a nature-rich curriculum.

This would only be feasible if all those in the teaching establishment were allowed to prioritize the importance of children learning through nature. This continuity of a child's natural interest would, I think, help them to trust and engage with school and each other in a more natural way. The children would all have a common interest, and one that they would naturally be observing all around them daily. We're a long way off this at the moment but it's a very healthy and hopeful vision and I'd like to think it could be possible. With home and school becoming nature-driven learning environments this would enable a child to remain curious and build on their early and established bond to nature.

I have seen that good communication with children and taking the time to listen and learn alongside them can be beneficial and educational. My own children and I have experienced this from their infancy and subsequently need little encouragement to communicate with or learn alongside each other as we continue to spend time together. They have the freedom to talk to those around them of various age groups and play at will.

Such confidence in their natural learning did cause a dilemma when it came to deciding if school was right for our children. In the end, as both children were really keen to try school and find friends, they initially went to the small local pre-school and then on to a primary school in the village where we live.

Their interests inspired imaginative and inventive play which they incorporated into most of their games at home or when they were at school. The knowledge they have gained over the years from playing and appreciating nature is good for us to see and this was later confirmed by their teachers, who recognized their significant interest in the world around them, mature approach and good general knowledge.

With their natural approach to learning running alongside their mainstream schooling they persevered for a number of years with the challenges, but then along came their biggest hurdle: homework. The worst thing about homework was that it stopped them from learning naturally through their play, and time and time again we would find ourselves reluctantly asking them to finish (or leave) what they were doing to complete their homework, and it became a battle.

This was a bother to us all and so I decided one warm Sunday afternoon that I wouldn't call my son in to do his maths assignment. I was already appalled that it had been set for the class by a local newspaper. Instead, I sat myself down with the instruction sheet and followed it. I had to flick through the paper and write down the weather for the weekend (for example). Even now I don't feel inclined to go into detail!

What I found interesting was that although I had found the homework easy my negative attitude obviously had an influence as I managed to get a few answers wrong. I just wasn't interested in doing the task and as a result I made mistakes, distracted by my own annoyance at having to do it and wanting to be elsewhere, just like a child in school perhaps.

Following the introduction of homework we would often find ourselves talking through schooling options with the children and we left them to decide when (or if) there would be a time to leave mainstream school to continue their natural learning at home.

All that a child finds interesting should be seen as relevant to their learning; only then can their knowledge gained be valued.

(My own observation)

Chapter Four

WHAT ARE WE THINKING?

Any parent facing an education dilemma knows that any decision made on behalf of their children isn't one that they can mess around with; no action should be implemented lightly or acted upon quickly in a willy-nilly fashion. Whether to home educate is a decision that needs to grow and develop.

The only possible downside to this natural progression of thought is the persistent interruption from those who seem intent on spontaneously giving you advice on why all children should be in school. Home-educating parents and their children are often put on the spot and questioned at random. This can feel like a very blatant invasion of privacy and these curious minds seem oblivious of this as they intently search for answers; completing their quest to find out exactly what you are thinking appears to be of the utmost importance.

This questioning can occur regardless of whether you are in the supermarket aisle, walking the dog or walking through town, and it can be uncomfortable and distracting. Many home educators who experience this will try to end these conversations as quickly and politely as possible. Discussing with others why my children aren't in school isn't something that benefits my children; however, discussing how children like to learn and the benefits they gain from spending time in the natural world is something we should all be talking about.

Parents may be curious enough to ask questions for a number of different reasons and it can often be difficult to briefly explain a decision that is the result of so much thought. A hesitation before responding could be misinterpreted as doubt and this may trigger them to offer unprompted advice. It could just be that the parent asking is looking for confirmation from you that the school their child is attending (and will remain in) is not the reason that your child is leaving, or they may simply not want your children to leave the friendship group of their own children. It helps to bear in mind that your own children will trust your judgement and your instincts; they will be observing how you act around other parents, family members and peers when it comes to discussing their education.

Having just written about unprompted advice I don't really feel I should follow straight on with some parental advice! But here it is: We made sure we spoke about educational choices to our children before anyone else and they've always known that they have a choice when it comes to where and how they learn; because of this we've always had an idea of how they feel about their education at any given time.

Making the decision to leave school and especially their friends was a time-consuming process. Some children need this time to think it over and adjust to the idea, and their parents will be focusing on them, hoping to ensure they all choose the best learning environment that circumstances allow. Deliberation is therefore personal and crucial in the process, and unhelpful comments can cause you to focus on others and not the ones that matter the most when it comes to making this decision. During this time I found it easier to distance myself from socializing in their school environment.

If you show your children that you trust them to learn naturally and you are on their side, they will recognize that you will always consider their needs first. As a result they will feel secure if it becomes necessary for them to politely defend their education.

I, as their parent, must continue to take the burden of any unprompted questions about my children's education, ensuring of course that my children understand why people may be curious. We still get questioned from time to time but overall we now find that people are intrigued and respectful of our decision. My children and I have grown accustomed to keeping our responses simple and polite. You do get used to the curiosity of others and I remind myself that it doesn't make a difference to my children's education if unexpected or inconvenient questions arise.

It is becoming more obvious to me that many parents are in fact interested in home education, and the research and evidence of how rewarding home education can be is very well documented. In contrast, they can also see the often negative and concerning news reports fed into our homes regarding the current school education system.

For my own family there was an enormous sense of relief when our children left their schools in September 2014 to continue learning naturally. As any parent would agree, getting out of the school system quietly with your children smiling and everyone's confidence still intact is what we all aim and hope for.

We have to face the fact that we all make decisions for our children and it can sometimes take courage to keep a child in school as much as it takes courage to walk your children away from an education that most of society sees as compulsory. As the limitations of school become more recognized and we discover and compare the growing educational resources online (like the wonderful Khan Academy[1] for instance), it's really no surprise that the number of home-educating families is continuing to rise. In our county alone there are over three hundred families that are now home educating. More parents are now making this decision as they take into consideration all educational options available and can see for themselves how children are being successfully educated at home.

Our children don't regret going to school as they made some lovely friends there and it enabled them to see clearly for themselves the different ways that children can learn. I think all children who are cared for and nurtured start school with an enthusiasm and interest for learning and they have to trust their school not to let them down. My children have to trust me not to let them down as I spend time with them in their preferred

---

1   The Khan Academy is a non-profit educational organization with the aim of providing a free, world-class education for anyone, anywhere. See www.khanacademy.org

learning environment at home, where they can experience free access to their natural world daily. They have become self-sufficient learners and their confidence in learning this way has grown with them. Doing my own work alongside them provides many ideal opportunities for us to sit down together. These days it takes little encouragement for them to join me and soon enough we are all tapping on our keyboards; they are learning to touch type, as this is a pretty useful skill in the modern world. Quite often the clicking of laptop keys stops as we pause to talk, observe or get distracted by the dog or wildlife; happy times, you could say.

I've found this book particularly easy and enjoyable to write because it involves two things I enjoy: being with my children and writing. If I was to journey back in time to visit the fed-up fifteen-year-old me clockwatching at school and ask, 'What do you want to do when you are older?', I would have replied, 'Be a mother, a writer of children's stories and live in the countryside.' So one could say I have achieved my goals as I'm writing alongside my two children in our rural setting.

Unfortunately society does sometimes see things a little differently and there have been conversations over the years that have led me to consider that some members of society view 'stay at home'-style parenting as an option for those less ambitious. This could be because there are more choices for women these days, and I do agree that this should be the case; after all, it's what I would expect for my own daughter – that she has the same career choices as her brother. But what happens to your place in society when you confess that you have given up work to look after your offspring? What makes society think that the most responsible, challenging and rewarding role of being a parent isn't worth leaving a job or career for?

I think most parents and role models would agree that infants and young children require daily attention, affection, communication, kindness, guidance, understanding, patience and dedication. Nurturing a child is a great responsibility and therefore naturally hard work. When our own children were infants we chose not to hand this responsibility over to somebody else, but many do for good and valid reasons. So it seems that however parents decide to nurture their children there is a need for justification as we jostle to secure positions in society that enable us to provide for our children. With some mothers choosing to stay in their career, some worried they would go out of their minds at home with only the company of an infant, others worried about the finances if they don't return to work and some just uncertain – what does this mean for today's children?

Some families prefer to rely on grandparents, or staff in playgroups, pre-school or the school environment when it comes to finding assistance in nurturing their children. Our schools have become multifunctional establishments which can offer childcare to children as young as two years old and provide after-school clubs to accommodate the working needs of their parents. So in a modern society, when do children get time to be themselves and play freely? When do they have quality 'home time' where they can choose to spend time outside with nature, play with siblings or have time to get bored?

Our natural spaces such as parks, woodlands, gardens and beaches are bereft of the sounds of children most weekdays throughout term time. In daylight hours children are keen to play and should naturally be out exploring the world around them. We should acknowledge these needs and reconsider where and how often we give children the freedom to explore new environments as part of their education. The familiar sound of children playing should be as natural to us as the sound of birdsong. If you are lucky enough to live near a school or are around when they let the children out into a fenced-off field or concrete playground to play, then you can still hear it.

Not everybody feels this way, of course, and a number of comments from other parents and family members have stayed in my mind over the years. These are typical of the type of comments that many parents of school-age children may hear from time to time as they walk across the school playground or when attending family events:

- 'I couldn't bear the thought of getting to my age and realizing I'd just been a mother all my life.'

- 'I couldn't stay at home all day – I'd just get bored.'

- 'I love my children, but I love them even more when they are in school or asleep.'

- 'I could hear him screaming from the crèche while I was in the gym.'

- 'They're going to that club after school tonight. I don't know what it's about, it's a club!' (Implying, perhaps, that 'any' club is better than going straight home.)

In fairness, these comments are out of context and one or two may have been said in jest. But what worries me is that parents may feel that it is important and more socially acceptable to say that there is more to life than just being a parent. They may feel they have been educated out of the realm of just parenting, and this certainly appears to be approved of in today's ambitious social groups. But what does it say to our children when we place such little value on the natural role of being their parent?

Interestingly the comments above are from mothers and not fathers, which could simply be because it's still mostly mothers who drop off and collect their children from the school environment. However, these roles can easily be reversed today and, of course, all families with young children will inevitably have decisions to make about parental roles. We should expect all members of society to be respectful and understanding of these decisions; currently, though, it seems we are often a little hard on each other and as a result parents have become accustomed to justifying their parental decisions.

With such diverse lifestyles there is not going to be one ideal solution that suits all, and in most cases it is considered and assumed that all childcare arrangements are made with the child's best interest at heart. So I think even though as a species we can be diverse in our approach to nurture we're still very similar when it comes to how we feel the need to justify (particularly to other parents) our childcare decisions.

And of course we can't underestimate the loyalty of children as they will naturally defend their own interests and take on board the views of their parents. They can also come to their own conclusions and if they're kept informed of all choices then they can participate in many decisions, from an earlier age than most would expect.

By regularly joining in with discussions that involve making decisions my own children have developed a tendency to calculate and weigh up the short- and long-term costs involved when making a decision.

EXAMPLE: My own children know (from regular family discussions) that the cost of purchasing a cello and having regular lessons is less than purchasing a top-of-the-range mobile phone and paying for its use. They have shown that they are able to assess all potential purchases this way by giving thought to the value and benefits of each item. They compare the cost against other items and think about the usefulness of any product, both in the short and long term. When it comes to making any choice or decision they now consider their options and compare alternatives. They were able to apply this thinking when it came to the short-term and long-term benefits of either a school education or their home education.

Therefore, my success as a man of science, whatever this may have amounted to, has been determined, as far as I can judge, by complex and diversified mental qualities and conditions. Of these, the most important have been – the love of science – unbounded patience in long reflecting over any subject – industry in observing and collecting facts – and a fair share of invention as well as of common sense.

Charles Darwin (1887)

Chapter Five

SLOW DOWN, SWITCH OFF AND SEEK ADVENTURE

Some parents may see the persistent pressure being placed on children (and indeed teachers) in many of today's school environments as a cause for concern. Many schools continue to focus and place emphasis on achieving fast, accurate and 'outstanding' results in a competitive and target-driven environment. It isn't any wonder to me that many teachers are leaving the profession and some parents are now looking to slow down the pace for their children in the hope of ensuring they can have a happy childhood and gain valuable knowledge in the process.

Although my husband Ian's work is office based and he isn't at home with us every day, he still finds the time to mention to the children the wildlife he comes across while going about his day and occasionally gets the opportunity to photograph it. Our children enjoy hearing about his days and he will often arrange time off to accompany them on fossil-finding fieldtrips and to the coast. They enjoy working and learning alongside him on these days and as a result they are now keen photographers too. I didn't realize in the early days quite how much my own knowledge in these areas would grow just by observing them observing him.

Ian believes that humans learn best when they are interested in something or if it's in their interest to learn it. Both of my children agree with this and they have just informed me that in school if you didn't finish early morning mathematics you would miss first break, so you had to get it done – fear of losing their break time was enough to get them going!

I think they are right, and learning through fear in a school setting seems to be an accepted way of learning. This surprised me, particularly as parents don't appear to be challenging it. In fact what you can find is that parents often side with the school and continue this fear-led teaching pattern at home when it comes to completion of homework; any preferred interest of their child can quickly become a recreational bargaining tool as the allocated homework takes top priority.

I have heard many parents discuss their children's lack of effort and interest in school or homework and how there are often tears over it (particularly with boys). I can remember one parent informing me that her son now considered himself 'too cool for school' and I acknowledged her bemusement at the time. It later occurred to me that even though her son had switched off to school he was still attending. His mother continued to make him go and he believed he still had to go. So for many families it appears that no other educational choice is considered; they seem to be unaware that there is even a choice. Schools and their teaching methods have become the naturally accepted way of gaining knowledge in modern society even though they remain a popular topic of heated debate amongst many concerned parents.

We also have the introduction of technology to consider when raising children in a modern society. Technology these days certainly has the attention and respect of many parents but I feel that young children also deserve the same level of attention and respect daily. Young children need to be (and enjoy being) in the natural world and their early interest should be considered relevant just for the health benefits alone. I think all children should be encouraged to understand and respect the environment that sustains them, in order to develop the human life skills they need long before we prioritize technology on their behalf.

My own observations have led me to strongly believe that technology should only be introduced once a bond to nature has been established, as this can then enhance and open up the natural world to them further. Learning this way can be adapted to include all 'school' subjects. They learn naturally as they explore the Internet (supervised of course) and build a more in-depth understanding of the world around them.

NOTE: One website that often springs to mind and always holds their interest is that of the British Geological Survey. It's fascinating and includes many hands-on science projects, such as how to make a seismometer out of a Slinky toy.

Children are keen to fit in socially and can be quick to follow trends. So when they find themselves confined in a school environment their parents may feel more inclined to provide them with the latest technical devices in order to help them keep up with their peers.

When it came to owning a mobile phone we preferred not to do this; instead we helped our children to come up with socially acceptable reasons why they didn't need to have a phone in school. We ensured they knew what to say by pre-empting situations and talking through scenarios beforehand, and this meant they were ready to answer questions from their peers with confidence.

Of course, helping them to understand why it wasn't wise to have a mobile phone in primary school meant they accepted the fact they shouldn't have one, and they didn't question it themselves. This understanding ensured they were not distracted by technology at an early age and enabled them to concentrate on their established interests outdoors and at home.

We did, however, provide them with other technology to enhance their interests – cameras, for example – and we were still aware of the importance of them being able to fit in with their friends. So we happily supported them when they asked to save up their pocket money in order to purchase a games console. It took them a while and they would regularly count out their money and work out how much they had left to save. It's now good to see them appreciating their purchase and playing online with their friends.

As a parent if you rely heavily on socializing and organizing your life with and around technology then your children will do the same. We form habits and routines that become a way of life, and as roles models we are continuously setting examples (good or bad) for curious young minds as they learn their behaviour from us. If a parent shows an interest in all things and a child observes this, then they, along with their parent, will have a reason to switch off a games console or computer. Technology is often provided to young children by their own parents so this instantly gives it increased relevance. The sights and sounds of the natural world can fade into the background simply because no value is ever placed on it. A child's young mind can become accustomed to being entertained, and this expectation will remain with them as they build a reliance on technology and develop a tendency to feel silly or disgruntled when they are sent outside to explore for no other reason than to get some fresh air or because it will do them good.

With many parents believing that school will teach children everything they need to know, and with an abundance of technology options to entertain them at home, a parent may assume that they have very little to do and therefore have very little involvement in nurturing them. With 'nurture through nature', once a bond has been established and at the appropriate time you can start researching and working online with your children. By communicating and working alongside each other they will soon see how technology today can be life enhancing. It's a fun, important and powerful tool and we can show them that we have it as a resource to find out about the world and our place in it. They will soon discover for themselves that the world is just part of a very fascinating universe as they carry on learning through their curiosity and interests. Introducing technology this way as an early research tool can lead them to see and plan new things to do, as it's in a young child's nature to absorb it all and they will naturally respect and protect all that their parents place value on. You can share and enjoy being part of their world where their interests can lead them down new paths. We shouldn't ignore or dumb down their enthusiasm to learn anything that interests them as they grow (with or without technology); we should encourage it daily.

Children like to observe the adults around them and learn as they focus on their own interests. They can choose to ponder or get involved and communicate as much or as little as any adult would. Sadly, I think it's become normal to be respected for what we have rather than who we are, and we all fuel this as a society, whether it's feeling the need to reel off our achievements or wave around the latest mobile phone. Cars can play an obvious and important role for many; the only car I ever really loved was one of the old family cars that we had when I was growing up. It was a beautiful Wolsey Hornet, a grey one with tatty and worn red leather seats. My sister and I would sit in the back (obviously!) and would turn around and kneel up to wave at the people behind. We fell off the backseat once when our mother braked hard and we got a telling-off. There were no seatbelt laws for those travelling in the back of cars in those days.

So, as I've just shown, we share memories and take pride in our belongings, and we care about how we come across to others and what they might think of us. We take care over how we come across and how we like to be perceived. Where we place ourselves in society plays an important part in how we feel when meeting others. If we stood face to face with a stranger we would try to place each other in a specific area of society simply because it's become a human habit to do so.

Is it then in our nature to judge others by their looks or parenting choices? Is it important to others how we choose to dress or where our children are educated? Do we really need to consider how and where we eat, shop, holiday and accessorize our lives? Not naturally, no – I think not. I think this has become the nature of our modern society. In terms of acceptance and survival it is only in our best interest to fathom out if people are a threat to us, or if we're going to like a person and get along with them and trust them to become acquainted with our family or social group. So what really matters is whether we are approachable and friendly, but in today's modern society it seems to have become more important to judge people's materialistic style. We may even adapt our own materialistic style to create a good first impression, perhaps in the hope of being accepted into a new social environment. It's sometimes difficult to concentrate on anything else simply because we are all still trying to get along in a ready-made materialistic environment and not a natural one.

If we faced a famine or a worldwide disaster then I think we would all come together and focus on the survival of humankind. Now is perhaps a crucial time, with many environmentalists and scientists believing that we have reached a critical point in regard to climate change, but unless we are told otherwise, as is our custom, we will all just assume we can keep hurtling along the same path gathering momentum by working hard as we aim for success in our man-made environments. There are many distractions for us, of course: and some of us will strive for leadership; others will shy away from the pace and become hermits; some will just make money while others spend it; many will turn to various sources of entertainment; others turn to food or alcohol (or both) for comfort. Long will it continue…but at what cost? I think we are all fully aware of the detrimental effects our lifestyle choices are having on our environments.

We could simply choose to slow down our pace a little and pay attention to what is going on around us in the natural world. This could make things easier for our own children and future generations. If we recognize our role and pass on any knowledge gained to the next generation, gently ushering them across onto another successful and productive road – perhaps one where they can still succeed but at a more enjoyable pace and which enables them to talk about the view – then just think: one day we could be regarded as the parents of the generation that started to turn things around.

To achieve this we simply have to consider daily how we come across when we nurture our children. The role of a parent matters and children need to see that the crucial and valuable role of parenting is not being ignored by modern society. Currently, rather than creating integrated communities we find ourselves mostly living amongst various pockets of social groups. Our style and behaviour enables us to fit into an area of society where we feel comfortable and can be ourselves. Often it's our adopted style and behaviour that determines how our own children come across when confined in large numbers in a school environment.

With all this in mind, understanding such diverse parenting styles can help children overcome peer pressure. Adults often have the choice to walk away from a situation if they become uncomfortable or are pressured to adapt their behaviour in any way. We can change our workplace if we no longer feel comfortable, or leave when we feel like a change. A child in a school environment cannot do this, and as a classroom is not a natural environment for a child, their education can sometimes take a backseat while this jostling for social acceptance is going on. My own childhood school was no exception and one piece of advice I was given to protect me from the social jostling was to 'Keep your head down and you'll get through it.'

Years down the line and I find myself home educating my children, discovering with quiet confidence that I should continue to follow my instincts and politely question well-meaning advice from family and friends. A friend of mine who was curious asked me recently, 'How do you know they are learning? You can't test them.' My response was, 'Why do I need to test them when I can see for myself or ask them?' We casually considered this as we moved the conversation along.

For some of us qualifications remain a sufficient measure of our intelligence, proof that we have done enough in our education establishments to succeed, but there are others who prefer to learn all through their lives without being tested or judged. As a society we need to appreciate that learning habits vary as much as people do, and both approaches have proved successful.

I consider an individual's education to be personal and because of this I don't feel inclined to test the knowledge of any person, adult or child. Speed of learning as a measure of intelligence isn't considered relevant in 'nurture through nature'. For this reason

I will never understand the push to apply pressure on any child in the hope that they will eventually be able to answer a maths question quicker than a child anywhere else in the world. As a species, it's obvious that we develop at different rates. I didn't need to look any further than Albert Einstein when it came to finding an example for this. It is well documented that as a young child he didn't thrive that well in the school environment. I can remember reading that he did in fact refer to this himself when he observed his own curiosity about things such as the universe. He would often become interested in subjects much later in his development than that of his peers, and could therefore, perhaps, give more time and thought to the matter than a younger child who had covered the same subject in school but had been encouraged to move on by their teacher.

This raises the question, 'How do we know what children are capable of naturally if we insist on trying to make them conform so early in their development?' Perhaps we should consider that some children are more suited to having time and patience to develop. We shouldn't assume all children are going to benefit by focusing on a curriculum; how can they remain curious if they spend a vast proportion of their childhood trying to provide answers to set questions that have already been repeatedly answered by so many others who have gone before them?

Perhaps that's why for some it becomes the seriousness of the race that leads them on to succeed; those who have happily conformed may be able to focus on the targets and compete. It would make sense that they would thrive in the mainstream school environment as they turn learning into a game of achieving goals. They would simply enjoy the race to thrive and become more accomplished at it. It would make for good future business sense and I can see how this could be of interest to some of the more competitive members of the class.

Unfortunately, though, the 'game' of achieving curriculum targets may not be something all children feel inclined to play. I believe that if left to their own devices many children would (in their own time) naturally set themselves aims and goals, but ones they can quietly work towards at their own pace. When it comes to discussing science in particular with my children, I will often highlight the work of 'maverick' scientists and how they made a difference by questioning further what others in the field had long accepted to be undisputable fact. Our children are learning from this; they appreciate that we live in a world where it can be good to politely question things a little further. Sometimes it can in fact be beneficial to take the time to observe the same things as others but from a different angle and from a less-travelled direction, as many historic figures have shown.

Questioning things is what children do naturally and often one question can lead on to a new topic or interest. We once spent the day as Vikings; it was my children's interest in Scotland and questions about dragons that led to this. We started off by researching (via technology) the history of Vikings and this paved the way for us to look further afield and overseas. We were soon back to discussing England and this led them to re-enact their own Battle of Maldon which further led to a discussion about J.R.R. Tolkien and the Anglo-Saxon language before finally preparing a Viking fish supper. The children planned this day well; costumes were needed and they were keen to limit the use of electricity. I have to admit I was a little thrown when they switched off my hairdryer...while I was still using it! This was amusing and it made me wonder what else they had in store, so from the hairdryer moment onwards they had my full attention and I was able to join in with their effort to ensure authenticity. Both children were fully absorbed throughout the day and this made it a success. I don't think any of us could have predicted that we would cover such diverse and interesting subjects.

NOTE: When left to their own devices children can often invent their own versions of popular games. My own children sometimes base their games on a topic suggested by me but mostly base them on their own interests and general knowledge. Just recently we had Shakespeare charades where they wrote out the titles of Shakespeare's plays onto little pieces of paper, folded them and then placed them into a box. We shook the box and then took turns to take a piece of paper and act out the play selected. This has also been played with many other subjects, including dinosaurs and various book titles.

They have created their own version of Monopoly, called Slothopoly; here the aim is to collect sloth cards and save up for sloth enclosures (instead of houses) and sanctuaries (instead of hotels). They each take it in turn to be the banker and this is a good boost for their maths skills. We all enjoy this game.

So we can see that children may have a preferred environment in which to learn. Some enjoy the race to succeed and like to get rewarded for their efforts while some may choose to have a more relaxed approach to how they learn. Consideration should be given to how individual children prefer to gain knowledge, and it's often worth reminding ourselves that children are watching and learning from us all the time. It is important for us to be aware of this as some (not all) parents today appear to be ignoring the nurturing process altogether. There are many factors to take into account when we consider how a child develops but it is well documented that we cannot ignore the importance of encouraging close bonds. If, as it should be, parenting was considered to be a highly regarded role and one that was respected by all members of society, then I think more provisions enabling parents to spend a greater amount of time with their young children may well become available. As a result, more parents would be given the opportunity to witness their children's natural curiosity and possibly also discover the benefits of nurturing through nature.

In time I hope all parents of school-age children will become accustomed to the educational choices available. Whether as parents we choose to work or stay at home, whether our children go to school or stay at home, these are personal choices for families alone to make. There is a lifetime of learning available to all of us if we feel inclined to search for it, and school can be part of it or not.

I have often wondered how young children feel, behave, learn and act in their multifunctional environments and whether society would benefit by comparing the education of those taught in groups (often in a confined and controlled school environment) against those taught alone or alongside siblings (in a less-controlled and more familiar natural environment). Over the years I have been able to satisfy my own curiosity by observing these two learning environments for my own children, and I hope the coming chapters will go some way in explaining my observations.

Nothing could have been worse for the development of my mind than Dr Butler's school, as it was strictly classical, nothing else being taught, except a little ancient geography and history. The school as a means of education to me was simply a blank.

Charles Darwin (1887)

Chapter Six

'PLEASE SIR, MAY WE HAVE SOME MORE NATURAL HISTORY?'

In this chapter I will be looking a little more closely at the current mainstream learning environment and the impact it had on my own children. Having been nurtured and encouraged to play uninhibited in the natural world, adjusting to learning inside a classroom was going to be a challenge, particularly for our son, who was first to try it.

One teacher, who our son was fond of, kindly brought to our attention the fact that he had been asking to go to the toilet quite often: every lesson in fact. It turned out that he was just stretching his legs; he would escape to go to the toilet and always return unprompted. She was also aware that he had been delaying coming in from playtime. I specifically remember his teacher's expression at the time and felt comfortable that she was amused by his behaviour rather than concerned by it. Things soon became clearer to her when she spotted him outside in the playground. He was looking up at the sky, and she took the opportunity to ask him what he was doing, to which he replied, 'I'm watching the birds.' From that moment on she became increasingly aware of his fascination with natural history and remained very supportive of his interest.

Our son would sometimes observe the birds and other wildlife at school, but as he went through the years these opportunities became few and far between and he soon found it more beneficial to quietly observe his interest at home. In Year Five he attempted to put natural history on the school agenda by putting himself forward to become a member of the school council. He prepared a presentation that included the idea of setting up a wildlife film club at his school. Friends and like-minded peers were supportive of his speech and he was elected as a member of the school council. There were also two teachers (his science teacher and his form teacher) who were in full support of the club. There was even some interest from other school council members, and so it all looked and sounded really promising. Sadly, lack of funding and resources slowed things down, to the point where the wildlife film club was deemed unfeasible to implement. Instead the members agreed to organize an afternoon nature trail but this failed to gather momentum and they slowly ran out of time. Undeterred, our son was re-elected onto the school council the following year and remained a member up until he left in 2014.

NOTE: It was early autumn when I once watched a female blackbird eat eleven ripe red berries, and I thought it was rather a lot for her slender size. Birds can't allow themselves to get too fat or they will slow down and become vulnerable to predators, but neither can they allow themselves to starve, so I had to assume eleven berries was just right – it's a delicate balance that they naturally sustain. Another time the children saw a pigeon having a shower; he sat on the tent in the pouring rain, lifting one wing up and then the other... I believe that humans are instinctively curious about the behaviour of birds and other species.

It was obvious to both of our children that the study of nature was a not top priority in their school setting; and it was when our children started school that we noticed they were becoming more fearful of spiders. I believe this developed from an accepted and general assumption in the school environment that everyone hates spiders, and some reassurance was required. I think we all naturally jump when we come across a large spider as they can catch us out by running unpredictably in any direction they choose and at a very fast rate. But the more you develop an understanding of their behaviour and become accustomed to it the more you can overcome any fear you feel when they surprise you.

I'm glad to say that even though my children became a little more apprehensive of spiders it didn't stop them from stepping in and protecting them. They came across many children who would willingly harm them. I would often sense their disappointment with the lack of respect shown to insects in the school setting. I couldn't help but feel that more consideration was needed by a majority of teachers and role models. If children were to see their teachers taking an interest and being mindful of nature daily by simply and enthusiastically acknowledging a spider in the corner of the classroom, for instance, then this would be a giant step in the right direction for that class.

We would often talk to our children about why schools didn't teach outside more often and why people didn't like insects, or why (on one occasion) one of their teachers left the room when she saw a picture of a shark. It transpired that this teacher had a fear of all marine life and so it was always discussed with the view that not everybody takes the time to understand the behaviour of spiders or sharks and sometimes you can have fears or feel anxious about them. As it turned out they already had an understanding of this and respected the fact that not everybody in their school environment had a shared fascination for the natural world. My own children would mention how their class went to great lengths to ensure this teacher (who they really liked) was protected from her fears.

One new addition to their primary school setting was Forest School, and when we first heard about it as a family we thought it sounded great. Playing in the woods with hot chocolate to follow: this could only mean one thing...fabulous times ahead! Initially they did enjoy it but over time they realized that they would just be going back to the woods for another Forest School session of whittling sticks and making dens, and it would once again be made clear to them that they were not to stray out of the area sectioned off by tape. They would be instructed where and when to explore, where to sit and when to regroup in order to listen to their teacher. They had logs to sit on and these were specifically positioned for them to see their Forest School teacher, who would often remain standing while they remained sitting. It became as predictable to them as their indoor learning environment.

I offered to go along to two Forest School sessions as a parent helper. Just prior to this I had gained some interesting knowledge on how to set 'pitfall' traps for insects. This idea came via a teacher from another school through her involvement in a nature club website that my children had joined, and an opportunity arose for us all to meet up with her at the Birdfair in Rutland. Our children remember this teacher because of her enthusiastic interest in wildlife. Her work was already being acknowledged by some of Britain's finest naturalists and she continues to teach in a mainstream school setting today. This teacher actively encourages wildlife into the school environment and I thought that the children in our own local school would perhaps benefit from some of her enthusiastic ideas – hence the pitfall traps, as these would ensure safe capture of the insects. I suggested that the children may enjoy setting these friendly little bug traps (pots) in the soil and my daughter's head teacher really liked the idea of it. We went ahead and planned for this to be done over two days, setting the traps on day one and returning the next day to see what insects we had captured overnight. I also had high hopes that we would then be able to identify them. The first day came and I set about digging traps with the children; in no time at all the session was over and everyone seemed happy. We were looking forward to being rewarded with lots of lovely beetles and bugs on day two. On our return, every trap had something in it, much to the delight of my daughter (and relief, for me). The head teacher was pleased and the children excited as we set about trying to identify as many as we could.

Our attention soon turned to one extraordinary and rather large beetle that was crawling along a child's arm, and it was at this point the little girl froze. I stepped in to reassure her and all seemed well; she was pleased to have an audience. Other children watched with interest as the beetle slowly crawled along; one or two of the children even held out their own arms in the hope that the beetle would crawl onto them. A teacher calmly appeared and took one look at the beetle and then one look at me. Although she was smiling her subtle body language had highlighted her subconscious reaction. I sensed that although she was acknowledging the beetle, it was probably because she felt she had to. Children can sometimes see the purity of reactions better than adults and in this case they may have also recognized that this was just a courageous effort by their teacher to lead by example. I knew better than to suggest she should take the beetle as I suspected she wouldn't feel comfortable.

Luckily our attention was quickly drawn away as the beetle took flight. Shortly after, the lesson ended and the children were instructed to tidy up and then line up, and were promptly handed a wipe to clean their hands in preparation for lunch. They were being moved along. I looked at the children in the line-up and imagined what it would be like if all teachers were mindful daily of all insects in and around the school. The children would have their curiosity fed every day by role models who shared their natural enthusiasm, with little effort required.

As parents we place our trust in schools and in turn our children place their trust in us when we encourage them to attend and listen to all they are told. If a child attends school with no bond or interest in nature they will not consider it relevant in the learning process. If the schools themselves continue to place such little relevance on what crawls or flies in the learning environment then we will continue to create a generation ignorant of the natural world. What is interesting is how we would acknowledge or react to the presence of a butterfly compared with that of a fly, for instance. To highlight this point I have included an extract from a book that my daughter refers to here at home.

Imagine that you are sitting at your kitchen table. It is a beautiful summer morning; the door slaps shut after the dog has pushed it open with her nose to go outside. As you take your first sip of coffee, a housefly that entered when the dog exited suddenly claims your attention. Like a tiny vulture, the fly circles above the table, slowly descending, until she lands close to the sugar bowl. The fly walks towards the bowl, and stops by a few grains of sugar that you spilled when you lifted your spoon from the bowl two minutes earlier. The fly inflates her proboscis and begins to dab at the sugar. As you watch this, you begin to feel a mild sense of outrage, not because the fly is stealing sugar, but because the fly's moist, spongy proboscis, now dabbing at your table, was recently outside, probably dabbing at dog feces or the rotting chicken in the rubbish. You wave your free hand at the fly; she jumps into the air and hovers nearby before quickly landing back at the sugar. You bring your hand rapidly down, attempting to crush the fly, but she is too quick for you. You put your coffee cup down, rise, and reach for the flyswatter, a tool that humans, with their big brains, have invented to crush flies. The flyswatter doubles the effective length of your forearm and so doubles the speed of your strike. The fly has resumed dabbing at the sugar. You strike. The fly sees the rapidly approaching head of the flyswatter. She jumps and begins to fly, but the broad head of your simple tool stops her flight and smacks her with enormous force into the table. Her internal organs, including her brain, are crushed beyond repair. A tiny marvel of miniaturized circuitry and engineering lies mangled on your table. In your own brain, the circuits that would trigger shame or remorse do not light up. You brush the carcass to the floor and step toward the door, where the dog is scratching to be let in. (Byers 2013, p.1)

There are many of us who own flyswatters and behave like this in front of children. We continue to brush off nature (literally) and show such little respect for many species as we go about our day and place our attention and curiosity elsewhere. By doing this we turn our children's curiosity away from nature as they continually look to see what is holding our attention. We really shouldn't complain when they spend far too much of their time indoors focusing on the technology that we provide for them.

Children can see for themselves how highly regarded technology is in their school, home and society. We could also be showing them that nature is full of curiosities (including our own species) and if we emphasized the importance of respecting nature as much as we do technology then perhaps we could inhabit our planet more sustainably.

Sadly, in most schools today a brief introduction to nature is all some children will experience, in the form of a mini-beast topic, gardening club or attending a Forest School session every once in a while. Children in modern society are encouraged to grow out of nature and some even have to hide or put their interest on hold while they concentrate on fitting in with peers and focus on subjects considered more relevant through target-driven initiatives.

DISTRACTION: It's now autumn and Douglas, our Border terrier, is busy digging up the squirrel's secret stash of walnuts. He has crunched and eaten two of them so far this week (the walnuts not the squirrels...although I'm sure he would happily crunch them up too!).

For us as a family there was one time when the significant benefits of learning through nature became acutely apparent. It was when our daughter became poorly; she was seriously ill and required the care of Great Ormond Street Children's Hospital in London. There was a need for her to be observed and monitored very closely and this was of course a difficult time for us all. During this time it was important that our daughter did not pick up any infections, so both children, with the full understanding of their head teacher, were kept off school and taught at home for six weeks. Our daughter could be closely monitored (by myself) at home and we made a decision not to 'school' our children at all during this time. Instead we just let them decide what they felt like doing and they would often choose to spend their mornings outside in the garden. We talked a lot about how they were feeling, as there were hospital appointments to attend in London and it was a particularly anxious time. Forest School was still exciting at this time, having just been introduced to them in their school environment, and they were missing out on the batch of Forest School sessions with their friends so we created a similar environment in our own garden and made sure they had hot chocolate.

NOTE: During this time we spent a great deal of time staring at the lawn. We hadn't lost our marbles – we were watching the incredible efforts of a mole as little trails and mud heaps painstakingly appeared. Our daughter became very fond of waiting for him and so it was a very sad day when we found 'Mr Mole' dead; he was lying peacefully in the garden and appeared to be untouched. His cause of death remains unknown (we like to think it was old age). The children and I buried him; he has been accompanied since then by our very own Mr Hamster. They are now side by side in the border just outside the study window with two flint rocks marking their resting place. (Recently our son casually asked his sister if he could dig them up and keep their skeletons alongside his own collection of dinosaur bones...she gave a prompt response and needless to say her two little furry friends remain at rest.)

During this time off school I was checking my daughter's temperature three or four times a day and keeping a record of it. Just prior to taking her temperature I would always stroke her forehead (a habit that remained with me for some time) as I began to know naturally if she felt too warm. With weeks of practice I started to accurately guess her temperature just by stroking her forehead, and we turned it into a game to see if Mummy was right.

This was a time of intense nurturing for both children as they relied on the reassurance of my husband, Ian, and me to help them; they received drawings from their best friends and remained busy, curious and surprisingly happy considering their circumstances.

In order to protect our daughter from infection (which may have confused any diagnosis) there were no visitors at all to the house. The children and I spent six weeks in isolation while Ian went to work and brought home the food shopping. They had each other, their interests and of course their wildlife-filled garden. The children naturally took all of this in their stride and played well; they were in their familiar environment enjoying their EPIC education and they were once again enjoying uninhibited access to their natural world.

After six weeks or so we were greatly relieved to find our daughter was well enough to return to school. On their return both children fitted straight back in as if they hadn't been away at all. Their teachers had been kept updated throughout the six weeks and their friends were excited and waiting for them to return. The time they had spent at home didn't feel like isolation: it felt natural. Neither of my children complained and they remained upbeat when those moments arose where they would describe or guess what their friends would be doing.

During this time of intense monitoring and nurturing I was able to clearly identify the needs of my children (now in their primary school years) and consider how, once again, they were benefiting from nature. I could also take the time to compare their learning environments. As my children became the focus of my own curiosity I understood that they missed their friends but not the confinement of a school. I affectionately hung around and monitored their play but also their emotional needs. Once again this highlighted for me just how much of a driving force nature can be when it comes to how human beings gain valuable knowledge.

Both children fell naturally into a familiar and secure nurturing environment where they could learn through their curiosity daily.

(My own observation)

Chapter Seven

GOODBYE SCHOOL, HELLO WORLD

Prior to our children leaving school the four of us as a family had had many long discussions about education, learning through natural history and maintaining friendships. Finally, with our minds made up, we felt able to discuss our home-education plans with close family members and friends. This was a little daunting but we were pleased to discover that most were interested in finding out how our children like to learn. What was also interesting was that all family members and friends were quick to comment on the alarming pressure being applied in our schools today, and this appeared to be widely recognized regardless of whether or not they had children currently attending school.

It became clearer towards the end of 2013 that it was more likely than not that our children would leave the schools they were attending, and so we focused on how they would say goodbye to their peers and their teachers. We agreed that the best time to leave would be at the end of the summer term in 2014. Some of their closest friends had known for some time that home education was a possibility and this made things a little easier, but we were keen to ensure that the needs of all the children involved were considered.

During the Easter holiday in 2014 we rather bravely declared ourselves ready to inform the school of our decision, and at that point it felt like we were united as 'warriors' as opposed to the 'worriers' that we could sometimes be. The letters were typed up ready to be handed in and we all went along together, just prior to our children returning to school for the summer term. We took the approach of informing the schools first and then contacting the parents of their friends shortly after. Once the schools (and their friends' parents) had been informed, our children felt comfortable talking freely about home education within their close friendship group, and all the children did a grand job of keeping it pretty much to themselves. They went about their remaining school days quietly, keen not to encourage questions – as to leave quietly was their preferred way.

As expected, the response from the schools was professional and polite. Our children's move away from mainstream school came at a time when all of the local schools were going through a major 'overhaul'. The current three-tier system (primary, middle and secondary) was to become a two-tier system (primary and secondary). This would mean a major change from the existing working structure that had been in place for many years. The primary schools would need additional classrooms to accommodate the extra pupils who would remain in their primary setting until the time came for them to attend secondary school. This would leave the current middle schools in the area facing closure by 2016.

Sadly, there wasn't enough money left in the pot to complete the entire process as quickly as was hoped, and following a general election the newly elected coalition government promptly put all funding plans in the area on hold. This caused further confusion, upset, uncertainty and chaos for our local schools. Some catchment areas had already part-implemented the changes, but not the ones attended by my own children and their friends. These schools were to remain three tier for much longer than anticipated while great efforts were being made to obtain additional funding in order to move forward.

The plans that were in place for a new secondary school were also put on hold because of funding issues. There was increasing apprehension amongst parents that the entire process could in fact take years to resolve. A number of the middle-school teachers decided to move on and it certainly appeared that morale in these schools was low. Parents were facing hard decisions about their children's education. Initially my husband and I attended the school review meetings but over time we lost confidence, along with many parents. It was an uncomfortable era of uncertainty for the children, parents and teaching professionals.

We live in a very rural area and any additional pupils in these primary-school settings also meant additional cars travelling to the schools where parking was already a concern. Local residents voiced their opinions on the additional parking needs and this also became a consideration for the schools. Extra classrooms (encroaching on playground space) along with funding and parking issues became important factors to address, and these were distracting. The children caught up in this review had to spend a majority of their primary years with no clear educational path ahead of them, and potentially missed out on the full attention of any teachers who also found themselves caught up in the overhaul.

During these uncertain times parents would quite often discuss alternative education choices, and it was during this period that I came across the work of Dr Alan Thomas. Through reading his research I developed the confidence to follow my own gut feeling on how my children were learning naturally.

There is clearly a dilemma for 'middle-of-the-road' parents who recognize the contribution of informal learning but who also fear that it offers no guarantee that children will acquire essential basic knowledge and skills. It can be very hard, on a day-to-day basis at least, to show that informal learning is working. At school, daily evidence of learning, usually in the form of written work, is an integral part of the system. Teachers in school regularly assess their pupils and are expected to know with some precision what they have taught and what pupils have learned. It takes courage to question let alone depart from the security of this highly professionalized system. Yet parents' own observations frequently pushed them towards doing precisely that.

Most parents might not have departed greatly from the security of structured learning if they had not also been influenced by their children. Because children are at home with someone familiar they are much more able to influence the way in which they learn. (Thomas and Pattison 2009, p.8)

As soon as it became apparent to the others that my own children were leaving their school environment it triggered a small ripple of interest amongst some parents, and once again some discussions about alternative education choices were reignited.

NOTE: Once we had set off along the home-education path we bumped into other families that were contemplating the same journey. They would sometimes trigger a conversation with confidence and clarity of thought regarding home education, while on other occasions they would show extreme wobbles of doubt. What slowly became obvious to me was how similar they were when it came to the long process of deliberating and protecting their children's future, and this remained evident throughout the extensive decision-making process. This suggests to me that the instinct to defend and protect our children remains strong when compared to the casual approach to nurture that we can sometimes adopt in our modern society.

Thus our children's mainstream schooling path had been filled with uncertainty and lots of deliberation, and I believe the issues faced by our local schools probably did make our decision to leave the system seem more acceptable to others. I already knew, of course, that natural history would continue to be the main focus in the education of my own children. I may have touched on this with other parents but I didn't share this information readily.

The time came to leave and during their last week our children took their autograph books into school and came home with contact details and messages from their friends, teachers and peers. They both enjoyed their last day and, having made a small group of friends, they felt reassured that their departure wouldn't leave their closest friends alone in the school setting.

NOTE: My son and his best friend have both kept their wands (sticks) that they used during their 'Harry Potter' era, and my daughter received a little owl ornament from her best friend which she treasures, and which stands on her 'school' desk at home.

One lovely teacher who taught my son for a year bumped into us recently and her smile was instantly warm as she said to him, 'I thought of you just the other day; they were weighing all the animals in London Zoo and it reminded me of you.'

This was a teacher I remember with fondness as she showed great enthusiasm towards our son when he made a model of the Natural History Museum (NHM) in London. He spent a term working on it even though he'd never actually been to visit the museum. This teacher was aware of his efforts and because of his continued enthusiasm (such as when he took his iguana puppet called Darwin into school for an assembly) the school agreed that our children could both take a day off so we could take them along to the NHM. Our son still has the model that he made (and his puppet Darwin) and we've been back to the museum many times since. This is a good example of how a school embraced a child's interest and relaxed the rules to accommodate it. Sadly this teacher has since retired early and left the profession.

Our children chose to leave school but they both have fond memories of their time there – as do we.

At the age of seven our daughter held her own assembly to raise money for Great Ormond Street Children's Hospital in London. It was an assembly where she could talk to her peers about her own hospital experiences. They were curious and so she had the opportunity to answer many questions. I remember the evening before that assembly and just how anxious she was.

We talked about making the final decision in the morning, as 'night thoughts' were not always the best ones. We would wait and see what her 'morning thoughts' were like, and then she could decide. Even with a good night's sleep she still found her morning thoughts to be anxious ones!

I left her at school that morning in the company of her head teacher. She had spoken in a kindly way to my daughter, reassuring her that she would be able to decide for herself whether to go ahead. The school hold their assembly at the end of the day and so she had another wait, but we both knew that her final decision would depend on what type of day it would turn out to be for her. I wondered about her throughout the day and when I went to collect her I felt nervous myself and hoped that everything had worked out well for her. As soon as I walked into the playground the head teacher came to greet me; she was smiling with her thumbs up! It was an emotional moment and I felt so relieved and grateful to the school for handling the build-up so well. My daughter greeted me looking very relaxed and pleased. Her face was glowing; she was pleased because her teacher had told her she was a good role model. As we walked back to the car together she mentioned that the children would be selling cakes the next day to raise money for the hospital and also how they had reacted so kindly to her assembly talk. They had been keen to talk to her afterwards, with one boy saying that he would be using his pocket money to buy some cakes.

Photographs were subsequently sent through of our daughter sitting at the front of the hall talking to the school about her experiences. This is a day we will both remember, but if you were to ask my daughter what her best bits about school were she would probably say the time she won all of her events on sports day and when she was awarded first prize in the school's fancy-dress competition dressed as a Viking.

One of our son's best memories from school would be the time he went with his year group on a school trip to Cambridge to visit a number of museums. Prior to the visit my son took the opportunity to ask his maths teacher (twice) if they could perhaps visit the Sedgwick Museum of Earth Sciences (a favourite place of his). His maths teacher took this on board and said they would have to wait and see.

During the day my son's group found themselves eating lunch with their maths teacher just outside the Sedgwick Museum. My son asked if they would have time to go into the museum and his teacher said that yes, they could go, and he sent my son over to check if it was open. It was, so his teacher then instructed the group to follow our son as he would be giving them a tour.

There have been many times when I would have liked to be a fly on the wall and this was one of them. My son can still recount the afternoon in such detail that I can picture them in the museum as we discuss it. He shared his knowledge with his peers and his maths teacher; this was one afternoon when he could talk about his interest freely. We were grateful, as this museum had been an unscheduled detour in recognition of my son's enthusiasm. We were fully aware that our son had spent most of his time in school trying to incorporate prehistory into his own topics and play; therefore we were pleased that on this day his efforts were rewarded. Our son contained his excitement that evening but we could tell he was over the moon. His friends and peers had asked him questions about the exhibits and he was able to share his knowledge and respond to their questions.

The last day of school was sunny, which they remember fondly as this meant they could enjoy their playtimes on the field. At the end of the day at collection time our daughter's head teacher came over to where Ian and I were standing and we said our goodbyes and she wished us well; she commented that our daughter had been smiling all day and we were pleased. We were saying goodbye to a parent when our daughter was released from the line-up and rushed over clutching gifts. We left the playground with her and she was full of excitement, telling us about her last day.

We walked to the pub to collect our son (he wasn't in the pub, it just happens to be next to his bus stop). He strolled along, the sun was still shining and his friends were waving to him from the bus. He casually crossed the road to meet us, waving back to his friends as the bus pulled away. He gently threw his dinosaur rucksack into the back of the car, just missing his sister (an old habit), and climbed in next to her where they eagerly caught up on each other's news as they chatted about their last day at school.

DISTRACTION: My son has just interrupted me to say to come and look as he has found Niagara Falls on Google Maps and he can see a UFO on there too. Perhaps I'd better go and see if aliens have in fact landed at Niagara Falls, or maybe it could just be a flying visit!

To force square pegs into round holes is never a sensible decision. Relabelling and pushing the pegs harder won't make a difference either. Hammering the pegs home could work but just how much unseen damage is done in the process?

(My own observation)

Chapter Eight

MOTHER NATURE... SHOULD WE?

Perhaps now, more than ever, we need to nurture and look after (or you could say 'mother') our planet. Caring for our planet should be just as important to us as caring for our children, as their survival relies on it; this is quite a thought and yet as adults we seem intent on destroying many of the world's natural environments before our children have even had the chance to truly understand or respect them.

My own children have come to understand how environments can sustain life by being nurtured through nature. If circumstances allow then this understanding and bond to nature can develop early, and this was certainly how it seemed for us as a family. I wasn't even aware of what was happening at the time, and I will now often describe it as being similar to that time in their development when they were learning how to walk and how to talk. They did this by observing and placing their trust in us, and we encouraged them by responding to their expressions and actions. I was not aware of their observations or my response: their bond to nature, along with being able to walk and talk, became apparent through seemingly effortless communication.

Learning to walk and talk is considered natural by society, and it doesn't occur to parents to question this. Most parents naturally encourage their children to walk and talk. We assume that most new parents will encourage their children to do this. If developing a young child's bond to nature was also considered by society to be a natural occurrence, then parents would be coaxing their children not only to walk and talk, but also to build on their bond with nature.

If I've observed children correctly then a very young mind developing under the wing of the natural world will, without any particular or obvious effort, remain a curious mind. This seems to be a balance that works and because of this I am going to emphasize again how important it is to incorporate natural history into their learning. As a child develops and grows with an awareness of the natural world they can learn above and beyond their favourite school curriculum subjects. They gain knowledge of their world and all its inhabitants and this can help them retain a healthy curiosity and a lasting enthusiasm for gaining knowledge.

It's understandable that a bond to nature can help children stay curious and mindful, and when faced with so many technology-focused environments, we could all benefit from establishing a healthy nature/technology balance. Introducing a child to nature before technology lies in the hands of us, their parents.

Currently there are many parents who have no obvious interest in the natural world. Perhaps as a young child their natural curiosity was ignored or they could have been 'nurtured out of nature' during later childhood. Either way, they may now find that their own children show little interest in the natural world.

I think that many teachers are faced with this, and the fact that schools aren't giving much relevance to it either just fuels society's ingrained ignorance of nature. Parents may not be at fault here; many of us did not study natural history in school, as presumably it was not deemed important for us to know the full joy, benefit and relevance of our natural world.

We remain a very trusting 'school-led' society and therefore we won't necessarily feel inclined to protect what our schools don't respect. We follow our leaders and so we seem destined to remain an ignorant society when it comes to understanding, protecting and respecting our natural world.

Nurturing through nature allows a child to build on their bond to the natural world and develop a further understanding of how they can learn from it, and protect it in the process. And it certainly needs protecting: many of our near-extinct species and environments require our urgent attention and all our children are watching to see how we, the adults who are responsible for their futures, will respond. It wouldn't take long to remind them that we inhabit an amazing planet. Just think, the next generation could develop a comprehensive understanding of the world around them to pass down to their own children. Perhaps it could even give them more to comment on when they encounter new acquaintances, moving on from just acknowledging the weather!

I think we all know that it's not in a child's best interest to see their parent ignore nature or dip in and out of it when it suits, and we can't just leave it up to conservationists, environmentalists and naturalists to update us and tell us when a species needs saving or that our children need to climb trees.

As a society we are often reminded that alarm bells are ringing and yet we continue to show such little attention to our natural world. This is once again highlighted in *Harmony*:

> It is very strange that we carry on behaving as we do. If we were on a walk in a forest and found ourselves on the wrong path, then the last thing we would do is carry on walking in the wrong direction. We would instead retrace our steps, go back to where we took the wrong turn, and follow the right path.
>
> This is why I feel it is so important to offer not just an overview of our present situation and not just a list of solutions. I certainly want the world to wake up to the fact that we are travelling in a very dangerous direction, but it is crucial that we retrace how this has come to be, otherwise we will not head onto a better path in the future. (HRH The Prince of Wales 2010, p.5)

I have taken these words of wisdom on board and shared them with my children and in return they enjoy sharing their own considered opinions and coming up with solutions.

The study of nature should not be seen as a recreational pastime and we shouldn't assume that something exists just to annoy, sting or persistently bother us. As a family we enjoy taking the time to understand nature and this has been part of our daily lives as our children observed from the moment they were born how we (their parents) could respect the natural world, learn from it and benefit from it, but to do this they needed to see us acknowledging it. Nature isn't a hobby for us: our children have always understood that all species are important and therefore we don't expect to be entertained by nature. It's not there for us when it suits, and nature documentaries enhance an existing nurtured interest and are not used as a chance encounter to trigger it.

It is obvious to me that we all like to be out in the sunshine; we all like to breathe in the fresh air on a summer's morning and feel the sun on our faces; we run our fingers through sand when we get an opportunity to do so; and we listen to the birds. Our children can see from this that we enjoy nature, but do they see us respecting it? How many adults react badly when an insect lands on them, or when they see that a weed has dared to appear amongst their borders? Fly killer, ant killer, wasp killer and weed killer can still be found in many homes.

When I was in my late twenties Ian and I went to see Monty Roberts, the 'Horse Whisperer', having enjoyed his book *The Man Who Listens to Horses*. I became very interested in the bond he developed with the horses in his care. He demonstrated how understanding what motivates a horse's natural herd behaviour in the wild enabled him to replicate the horse's methods of communication through his own body language; mutual trust was gained, resulting in a willing partnership between horse and man. Monty Roberts refers to this technique as 'join up'. We enjoyed the demonstration and left the arena feeling incredibly moved by what we had seen. His bond and the kind technique he used in gaining the horses' respect and trust were clear for us all to see. His written work highlights his respect for horses but also brings to our attention the shocking impact that human cruelty once had on horses when used (by many) to enhance their strength:

> The horses had no answer to his cruelty, had no voice. But... they did have a language. No one saw it, no one tried to see it, but it was there then and it's still the same one now. It's a language that's been around for 45 million years and has remained virtually unchanged. Just to put this into perspective, mankind has been on this planet for only a few hundred thousand years, and already his language has fragmented into thousands of different tongues.
>
> The absence of communication between man and horse has led to a disastrous history of cruelty and abuse. Also, it has been to our detriment. We haven't captured the willing co-operation of the horse nearly as much as we might have done, and that is our considerable loss – both in emotional terms and with respect to the performance and work we might selfishly gain from them.
>
> It's a balance which I've been happy to try and redress during a lifetime's work with horses. (Roberts 1997, p.345)

I do often wonder why (as a species) we continue to show such little respect to so many species. I was curious to find out more and so I looked further into human nature, which will be the focus of the next chapter.

DISTRACTION: My daughter has just informed me that we have a swarm of honeybees looking for a home in the garden. I can see them, and stepping outside the noise just hits me: it's incredible. Douglas is showing an interest. I'd best go and lure him in with a 'confident cream', more commonly known as a custard cream. It only became a confident cream when my daughter needed a confidence boost and I suggested a custard cream biscuit may help... I would just like to point out that I don't make a habit of filling our daughter (or our dog) with confidence that often!

The bees are in! They've found a home under an old bike ramp, nestled in the border at ground level, and it's nice to have them around (although it's a bit close to the tent!).

Doug is in and he is buzzing; no really, he is literally buzzing...

Quick update: One game of ball can rid a dog of two angry honeybees.

NOTE: Other important nature 'events' over the last week: Sadly, we came across a dying dunnock in the garden; he is now awaiting burial. On a happier note, our pied flycatchers have returned safely from Africa and are extremely busy; they are at this very moment renovating their nest. Each year they take up residence in a climbing rose on the side of the house. They are not alone as the wrens have moved in next door on the trellis, and across the lawn we have a high conifer hedge full of 'far too happy' pigeons. This denotes that spring has certainly sprung this year, probably enhanced by the fact that the garden is so overgrown.

The doors and windows are now open, and we have the sound of honeybees and birdsong providing the background music to the children's learning on this beautiful spring day. That sounds a little sentimental; actually...no, it all makes perfect sense.

The grand way to learn, in gardening as in all things else, is to wish to learn, and to be determined to find out – not to think that any one person can wave a wand and give the power and knowledge.

Gertrude Jekyll (1899)

Chapter Nine

HUMAN NATURE... A DIFFERENT KETTLE OF FISH

We consider ourselves to be a species of great intelligence, and we are indeed capable of great things. But I have to say that I do find some elements of human nature particularly difficult to explain to my children. In their early years I found myself sometimes feeling ashamed when having to explain some elements of why humans behave the way they do. I realized early on that I could not keep defending the actions of other human beings, particularly when it came to (in no particular order) the destruction of environments, neglected populations and how we continue to push ahead – regardless of whether we are leading other species and potentially ourselves to the edge of extinction. This is inexcusable behaviour when seen from a child's perspective.

We hope and expect that our children will behave well and show respect, but they watch and learn from us and so they see for themselves (via the technology we provide for them) just how much devastation we can cause and how little we acknowledge this as we go about our daily lives.

We are often advised to ignore our children's bad behaviour and reward the good. Yet as adults we insist on reporting and talking about the bad behaviour of others constantly; good deeds are rarely reported. Tragic events are broadcast into our lives daily and we are reminded that many atrocities happen through a simple lack of respect for and understanding of each other and the world we live in. We are kept informed of bad behaviour and are regularly updated with regard to the latest death toll following any tragic event.

If my children hear a 'dramatic' report (not just nature related) then I take the time to discuss it and talk it through with them, ensuring they have an understanding of why it may have happened and what triggered it. I also highlight any good that could possibly come out of the situation. By doing this I hope to ensure they have a balanced view and an understanding of all current issues and why they may have occurred or are still occurring. So it can be a little frustrating when a news reporter describes a horrific crime in detail or depicts the person responsible as a 'monster', for instance. It's not in a child's (or anybody's) interest to have news presented this way. How as a parent can you explain to a young child why somebody has been described as a monster? It takes careful consideration to help them build an understanding of such descriptions.

More mature and sensitive reporting of events is needed to ensure the innocence of childhood is respected; currently you have to be a vigilant and determined parent if you want to keep the innocence of childhood alive in today's technology-driven society. A child's vulnerability is being ignored, and these days they could often be in a position to see or hear inappropriate and dramatically reported headlines that are designed to shock and hold the attention of adults.

In more recent years my two children have picked up on my own sense of frustration over the lack of balanced reporting of views and news, and they now suggest I don't watch or listen to it. 'Just turn it off Mum,' they say, perhaps followed by 'What was it about anyway?' So we still discuss it and they often remind me that the reporting is rarely a balanced view. I'm finding more these days that my children do now comment on the way in which an event is reported. They see all sides of an argument and take it upon themselves to share their balanced views with me. And so, instead of concentrating on the damage to the environment, I aim to point out the good work being carried out globally by those who are fully aware of their own purpose on the planet and who strive to sustain a future that works for all its inhabitants.

My children's home education is enabling them to ask about or research good (or bad) news if they wish. For example, they can learn how many people or animal species have been helped through fundraising for charities, for instance when they manage to increase some habitats for endangered species. We can discover together how much habitat is remaining for a particular species and if the numbers are going up as a result of human effort across the planet. We see communities communicating with and educating each other and people working hard to make a difference for our common interest in the natural world.

Our children are growing up knowing that it's important to support those caring for the planet's inhabitants. An awareness of the work carried out by wildlife charities was introduced early on in their development, and over the years both children have adopted a number of animals across the world and continue to gain knowledge through the newsletters they receive and via the charities' websites. They have learnt about the animals' habitats and plight. Over time they have seen reports and have been kept updated on the effort involved in turning situations around for many species. One of their adopted animals, Douglas the Hippo, was successfully returned to the wild through the efforts of supporters of the charity Born Free.

We care about protecting the rainforests and remain aware of the long-fought campaigns to save them. My children were also made aware recently of the impressive campaign by the World Wide Fund for Nature (WWF) to gain support in protecting the Great Barrier Reef; they subsequently heard about the overwhelming response and how this particular campaign was successful (for now).

Of course, once again we are not alone with our fights and plights, and for many species the natural world can be as hostile as it is beautiful, but one thing we can all learn from is the natural behaviour of all species. We all share this world and survival is our ultimate aim, but only the 'luckiest' of each species will live to reach their expected age. My own children have developed an understanding of this and they have watched many documentaries where hungry predators and their prey go to great lengths to survive. They have also witnessed the fight for survival in their own garden: the sparrowhawk and the pigeons, the fox and our hens. These events can be difficult to observe but become valuable life lessons all the same.

Over the years I have seen how my children's young human minds have been able to process and absorb all that nature has shown them. They can accept spiders darting about in their home environment and appreciate the effort involved in making their webs. They can understand how a baby fox may enjoy a meal of their own pet hens. Many of us are tempted to 'free range' hens as part of keeping animals humanely and as naturally as possible but it's worth noting that much of our garden was destroyed during the 'Can we let the hens out?' era. They are brutal in the borders and their dust-bathing areas are still visible today, and then there's the time we had a red mite infestation... So our garden has grown to be this way simply because our children, our domesticated animals and nature have developed it. It wasn't planned – it just happened – and it's an environment where children and nature interact and benefit each other in the process.

A couple of observations on how wildlife can introduce itself into your world:

- It helps of course to welcome nature in and we have trees, hedges, nettles, thistles, the odd bit of wheat and other strands of crop that have been blown or carried in, moss-covered log piles and many, many weeds. We also have wild flowers in our overgrown patches. As a result butterflies lay their eggs on nettles, goldfinches enjoy the thistles and we have beetles, spiders, slugs, snails and ants that are just everywhere! Ants, I find, are particularly amazing to watch... I once cooked spaghetti Bolognese alongside what could be described as an armada of ants. They appeared from behind the fridge on the warmest summer's day when the time was right for them to fly; sadly one or two flew into the sauce.

- If you've ever wondered, as I did one evening (while reading Harry Potter to my young son), why a large sleepy wasp should suddenly appear out of nowhere, when it's dark and out of season in a bedroom, it'll be because you disturbed its hibernation and it would no doubt be a potential queen. They like to 'sleep' nestled inside the puckered band along the top of your curtains. I discovered this and went on a quest around the house the following morning to count them; I found around twenty-two hibernating wasps. I did eventually get stung as one had nestled into the pocket of my daughter's dressing gown and I happily scooped it out assuming it was a hair clip. It was a horrible dawning for me as it stung and then clung; I watched as it hung on for dear life as I tried to shake it free from the end of my thumb.

We talk to our children in depth about these 'odd' occurrences and many other curiosities of nature and wildlife. They have become aware of the world's beauty – it's symmetry, art, landscapes, colours – and they naturally try to work out the science behind what they see, feel, hear or smell. They identify shapes and they count many things; they also age things; they draw and write signs for their habitats and games outside; they measure out the sizes of dinosaurs and other species; they wonder what it's like to live in other environments and to live as other species do; they guess the weight of things; they gain an understanding of geography and historic time lines and tell us what they think; they imagine and describe what it's like to live in our oceans; they study habitats and the temperatures required for different species to survive; they question how planets, suns, moons, black holes and galaxies are made; and they try to comprehend travel speeds and distances. They ask why and how we come to have natural disasters, extreme weather, tornadoes, landslides and earthquakes. They can find out about these things whenever they feel inclined to ask and, having recognized how repetition naturally plays a major role in their learning, they both know they can question an area of interest as many times as they need. A similar question may arise the same day, the following week, the next month or even a year later and then they/we rediscover it all over again and with the same enthusiasm.

NOTE: Our children (and I'm sure many children) have developed a habit of identifying animal shapes in cloud formations. As a family we have identified many cloud dinosaurs, a dragon, a turtle and even a bunny on a motorbike, and will often point these things out to each other. This can be amusing and educational as inevitably conversations like this can lead on to discussing how clouds form or what type of conditions are required to create storms, and so on. Bubble bath is also an excellent way of encouraging children to use their imagination as they play, forming shapes and attempting to create as many animals as they wish.

My children have studied how animals nurture their young and we talk about the birds and the bees. This is easier to do if they have a clear understanding of nature. My children had many questions to ask when they spotted two rhinos mating at the zoo. This quickly became an in-depth and impromptu lesson on 'how baby rhinos are made'. All subjects can be covered through nature; it really is the most amazing 'school'. One project can lead to another and this becomes a joy to watch as their research skills become relevant in everything they do. When they have developed that bedrock of understanding (see, geology!), then this is the time to introduce technology. Researching time lines is educational but constructing a time line in 3D using Minecraft on a computer is even more exciting. This enables them to recreate specific periods in our Earth's history using plenty of imagination and the 3D building blocks, and if they enjoy the process, they will remember it. This is where we see modern technology enhancing their learning environment.

NOTE: Recently we discussed the Mars mission and the cloning of mammoths (both exciting of course) and I asked my children why we (humans) should go ahead or why we perhaps shouldn't. The discussion focused immediately on how we were currently treating our elephant populations, and they both came to the conclusion that as our existing elephants need protecting, then we should perhaps concentrate on making things right for them first. Although they both agreed a baby mammoth would be amazing, neither felt encouraged by the thought of experimenting with either species, as it may require placing a mammoth embryo inside a female elephant. They also made the point that we (humans) may not be able to protect the mother and calf in the long term. Human behaviour was also the main concern when it came to discussing the Mars mission; they once again felt that we should concentrate on getting it right here on Earth first before we journey to other planets and risk destroying those. I think many children would have answered the same way about these two issues, and I find that an encouraging thought.

Many parents may already realize how shocking our treatment of the planet must seem to our children. After all, it's they who will have to bear the consequences of our actions in their future years. It's such a terrible shame; as a species we could have complemented our planet so beautifully. Perhaps our children and their children could get us back on track; the current generation should certainly be encouraged to believe they could still make a difference.

There are cultures and communities around the world that recognize the importance of protecting forests and other natural environments. They share an understanding that these are environments that are vital for survival and as such they ensure their children understand and respect them as a way of life; they learn and live with nature.

Working with nature and watching out for the warning signs that nature sends should be something we all consider naturally. This could have a number of benefits, as other species may have more senses (or at least are better tuned in to their senses) and this may enable them to survive when the wrath of nature storms in. I would encourage children to remain mindful of the behaviour of birds and mammals, or any species they are curious about. We may not be the most intelligent species when it comes to sensing extremes in our weather and protecting our young from natural disasters. Perhaps we just need to take a step back and look again more closely at how other intelligent species nurture and share their wisdom with their young.

 NOTE: I remember one time when our family witnessed a change of behaviour in our garden birds. It was during the eclipse, and we had set up a camera to record our home and garden during the event. It was mid-morning and we ensured we were outside together; sadly it was a cloudy day and so we were unable to (safely) view the eclipse itself. Instead we found ourselves watching the birds as they flew across in little groups to roost in the trees that surround our home. This behaviour was triggered by the false dusk of the eclipse and the area fell silent as the birds temporarily stopped singing.

Parents should not underestimate their children's ability (or their own) when it comes to gaining knowledge this way. We all learn by observing and responding to the behaviour of others, and with this in mind we should consider how past generations and our own families' histories may be of interest to our children, as memories of the past will enhance their learning and give them a strong sense of self, family and belonging.

I became aware of my grandfather's history through discussions with him and other family members, particularly about his role in the bomb disposal unit during the Second World War. Casualty numbers were known to be particularly high in this unit, so he was considered lucky when he suffered only serious leg injuries and permanently impaired hearing as a result of the blast he encountered. A bomb had detonated unexpectedly as he and his comrades approached; he found himself to be the only survivor of the blast and these injuries took him out of the front line of the war.

I can still remember him showing us the shrapnel scars on his lower legs and telling us how he was subsequently sent to Egypt to recover from his injuries. He became an army cook there and I think his time spent in Egypt helped him in many ways. When the war ended he decided he would walk back home, travelling over two thousand miles. I didn't question why he would want to do this and it didn't occur to me to ask. I always felt I understood why he would want to walk back; I assumed with the fear lifted and the quieter sound of freedom to adjust to, a walk home inhaling nature would help to ease the pain of traumatic memories. I always imagined that this would be more appealing than any other option and was more of a human need than anything else.

It was my mother who told my sister and me about the loss of his comrades as, like many others who returned from those times, my grandfather didn't talk of the horrors of war; he kept those memories to himself. Instead my grandfather told us about his recovery and the friends he had made while in Egypt.

My mother later told me that he had indeed made two very good friends and they had called themselves 'The Three Must Get Beers'. I saw a photograph that had been taken of them during that time and they had their arms around each other's shoulders, smiling for the photograph, and it was good for us to see this.

The knowledge of what my grandfather had been through had an impact on me as a child. I would look through the photographs he had kept of the service held for the many young men killed on 'the day that Grandad got blown up', as we would innocently refer to it. I understood that young men just like him didn't come home and so these experiences stayed in my young mind. If circumstances allow then we can all learn about past events from our own families and our own history. I learnt about the sadness and hardship of war in the company of my own family; I didn't enjoy learning about it at school.

In his later years my grandfather focused on what was important to him. He returned to his old love of growing vegetables, repaired old mantle clocks in his shed and spent his time caring for my grandmother and walking his dog. We would visit them every weekend and my sister and I would stay with them during the school summer holidays when our mother returned to work part time. I have many fond memories of being with him that I can now share with my own children.

These days we see many grandparents bridging the generation gap and having considerable input into their grandchildren's lives. I can remember my own grandfather cooking for us; he could make a wonderful Yorkshire pudding and as a result my mum was able to make them for us, so I could then observe how to perfect a good 'Yorkshire'. In time my children will observe the knack and long may it continue...a future of puddings to look forward too.

Through our many actions and recollections children can obtain further skills and knowledge; a conversation about a great-grandparent can lead (as in my own family's case) to an interest in their experiences and the countries they encountered. As a parent I have fuelled these discussions, and it's more likely than not that if we all looked a little deeper into our own family history then we would continue to find surprises.

Over many years and on a number of occasions when I have shown courage my mother has said to me, 'That'll be the Douglas in you.' She is referring to the Black Douglas clan in Scotland, as my great-grandmother was a Douglas from Ayrshire, and some of her sayings and stories have led us to understand that we are related to Archibald 'the Grim' Douglas (3rd Earl of Douglas). The evidence is in our family tree and so when I first heard of this it was of great interest, but the only problem was that no family member could remember the whereabouts of 'the tree'. I am about to resume a quest to find it and this amuses the children, as currently we think it is somewhere in the south of England. Anyway, the search continues and it remains a nice idea, a family myth perhaps.

In the meantime, however, I was not going to leave the whole idea of being related to this remarkable Scottish clan dormant and as a result I've latched onto it and we now adorn our home with items of a 'Douglas' nature. I am now the proud owner of a very long and itchy (being 100% wool) Douglas tartan scarf, and when it came to the naming of our Border terrier, well of course, we chose the name Douglas.

Our children like to talk to us about the Douglas clan and we've read about how Archibald the Grim's father, Sir James 'the Black' Douglas or 'Good Sir James' as he was also known, was associated with Robert I (Robert the Bruce). As a result of this interest we have discovered more of 'our' Scottish clan's history and the castles they inhabited. It's all very exciting but no doubt I'll just turn out to be the product of a 'bastard' heir somewhere along the line and all my vain imaginings will be promptly laid to rest.

To keep the balance we researched and found out a little more about my husband's ancestors; we discovered that one line (on his father's side) came from Fowey, in Cornwall. This line has been traced back to 'a gentleman of independent financial means'. We're not quite sure where this will lead us but, once again, it will be interesting for our children to discover their past.

We often find ourselves talking to current family members about past family members and researching our history in Cornwall and Scotland. This helps to build a picture of their ancestors (and boost my children's knowledge of the geography of the British Isles). This talk of other family group members is relevant as it was through my research (and watching natural history documentaries with my children) that I became acutely aware of the resemblance that my own upbringing and subsequently that of my children had to that of other intelligent mammals.

Highlighting again how I couldn't ignore the value of knowledge gained from family members, I remember times I was specifically 'taught' by other members of my own family group:

- When we were young my sister and I would visit our grandparents and we discovered that our grandmother had a great deal of patience; we know this because she taught us to knit. During our visit she would retrieve and place down in front of us a large bag stuffed to the brim with balls of brightly coloured wool. We would politely wait for permission before setting upon this bag, tipping it out and batting the balls of wool around. When the excitement had passed my grandmother would then hand us a pair of six-inch nails each to practise our knitting skills on. Only when she was aware that she had our attention would she start to knit. We would then concentrate, observe her technique and copy her actions.

- My aunt (from Australia) first came to visit many years ago with my uncle, but her visits were to become more regular following the sudden death of my father in 1989. My aunt became a welcome guest each summer and during these times I would quietly observe her cooking skills. I still use her techniques in my own cooking today.

I was able to gain knowledge from my elders (just as elephants do) through observation and repetition: they didn't tell me what to think or do; I just naturally chose to follow their lead and take on board any encouragement. Children naturally develop an awareness of skills and can choose to incorporate them into their own education through observation and repetition.

I often wonder if we (humans) instinctively recognize animal behaviour in our own. Since childhood I have always associated the word 'matriarch' with elephants, and as a result I think of their behaviour whenever my own mother refers to herself as the matriarch of our family. As their grandmother she has a great deal of time for our children; she recognizes their interest and feeds it beautifully. As I write this she is currently flying back from Australia, having just visited my aunt. Their friendship bond is a strong one; as a family we owe my aunt our thanks; she was the only one who could calm down Poppy, our Jack Russell terrier, when she went off the rails following the death of her master, my father. My aunt and our dog developed a 'mutual understanding' when she first arrived. They did eventually develop a bond and became very fond of each other, and I'm sure this had something to do with the little bag of pick 'n' mix sweets my aunt would often pop out to Woolworths for.

My aunt was a great help to us; she calmly distracted our dog and filled the house with smiles (and cooking aromas), but beneath the surface we were still getting over our loss. She knew this, of course, but took us in her stride. She flew in each summer and observed the 'not so nice' times becoming the good times again as our lives got back on a new track. Eventually my mother and my aunt started to holiday together in France and Italy. I would then be left to finish the pick 'n' mix with the now well-behaved (sort of) but still very much in charge terrier, Poppy.

I think children are able to develop an early sense of maturity when they socialize within the family group and I have seen this develop in my own children. By regularly communicating with the adults in their lives they have learnt the patience and maturity they need to communicate and they are respectful of others' feelings; they become accustomed to observing the reactions and behaviour of others. A young child who spends time around all age groups will develop an understanding of emotions and manners fairly early in their development. This becomes apparent when they start to question why people say and act the way they do. They are developing an awareness of body language and subtle facial expressions. It helps of course if a parent or role model is able to take the time to explain why people might say or do the things they do (good or bad).

What has been most fascinating to observe is that although my children spend time with older members of the family they still retain their natural instinct to play at will; this continues long after their peers in a school environment have been encouraged to grow out of observing nature and no longer feel inclined to play freely. My son noticed this happening around the age of ten: the children in his year group seemed more inclined to walk, talk, sit or, for some, just behave badly within their own friendship groups at break time.

What I really hope to show by looking at all aspects of nature and sharing my own experiences is how balanced life can be when we include family and nature in the education of a child. I have found that parenting needn't be difficult if we recognize the importance of all aspects of nature in this way. Even if parents have very little spare time they could still recognize the benefit of telling their children about the nature they have observed during their own day, by simply keeping a mental note and reporting back what they have seen to their children. A young child will soon develop a habit of doing the same in return, especially if they know their parents are going to ask them about their day when they return home. They will have gained an understanding that what they see in nature could be interesting and relevant to their parents.

We can readily retain an abundance of subject matter but if we do not call on that knowledge repeatedly or often then we will not retain it for long or even at all. (Hence remembering commonly used phone numbers but requiring intense revision prior to school examinations.)

(My own observation)

Chapter Ten

THE DEAD ZOO AND OTHER CURIOSITIES

The Dead Zoo is probably better known as 'the fish counter' in any supermarket but my children have always referred to it as 'the Dead Zoo' and it still holds a fascination today. When my son was very young he became particularly interested in the squid and was rather fond of it. Each visit he would ask if he could take the squid home and put it in the bath, and every week my answer was no, mainly because of my 'squid ignorance'. Is it safe to play with a dead squid? I had no idea at the time and so we moved on – but I didn't forget.

So we became regular tourists at the Dead Zoo, but on each occasion I felt that perhaps we shouldn't stay too long or show too much enthusiasm over so many dead creatures, and I found myself naturally observing the assistants as well as the enthusiasm of my children.

One afternoon (when we were gazing at the squid) a kind-looking assistant did venture over to us. I braced myself, ready to apologize for my children's interest and enthusiasm; after all, there were so many poor dead creatures. But she wasn't looking at me – she was smiling at the children and I watched with trepidation, as I didn't want anyone to ruin their enthusiasm. I needn't have worried. In fact, I could have hugged her...she was talking politely to them about the squid and they were all ears, especially as by now she had the squid in her hands and it was slipping all over the place. Then she did something even more amazing, something they can still remember: she showed them its beak! The fabulous lady actually showed them all the interesting bits of a squid and explained how they had also removed its ink sack. We saw bits I didn't even know it had, and it was fascinating. It was wonderful: this stranger for just one moment became an educator; she had engaged with my children and it got me thinking.

Having accompanied both of my children on school trips I was often able to predict their behaviour and that of their peers. If the Dead Zoo had been a school trip then instead of feeling able to focus and pay attention to the assistant (and the squid) my children would have unexpectedly found themselves taking a step back from the counter. This wouldn't be because the assistant or their teacher had asked them to move, but simply because some of their fellow class members would have expected to be the ones at the front, not necessarily because they were being mean, but because of a developed habit and an expectation of getting to the front and being the ones to see it first.

Sadly, this dominant behaviour is often allowed to develop and the habit of pushing in can be seen daily in the school environment when the children are asked to line up. This expectation to be at the front could be interpreted as part of the natural pecking order. In many situations this may be the case, but I don't think this should be assumed. Sometimes there can be subtle similarities between being overly enthusiastic and being dominant, and this should be identifiable in school environments. It's often the case that when the group of children at the front start to disperse, the rest of the children can feel comfortable enough to step forward in the hope of getting a glance before being moved along themselves.

On one occasion I arranged for the 'quieter' members of my daughter's class to come to her birthday party at our home. They greeted each other happily and after ten minutes or so they were comfortable enough to explore outside together as a group, and from that point onwards they were all joining in and talking amongst themselves. Another parent commented on this, as it surprised us. We weren't expecting them to be quite so loud and it was good for us to see. Away from the more dominant behaviour of some of their peers they were able to have a voice. They were soon inventing games that could be played outside in the garden, and that's where they chose to spend the rest of the afternoon.

DISTRACTION: We have a sparrowhawk in the garden. Actually we don't now but we just did; it has left a pigeon by my car and is currently sitting in the tree top waiting for the coast to clear before returning. The pigeon isn't moving and it's obvious to us that's it's dead, as there are lots of feathers flying around. Something must have disturbed the sparrowhawk's mealtime... I hope it returns or I'll have to scoop up the remains of the pigeon. The children, the dog and I are all watching and waiting from a distance.

IT'S WILD

We have a number of regular visitors to our garden, including a spring visit from 'Duck' and her brood of ducklings, much to the delight of the children and our Border terrier, Douglas. Chickens once ruled our world until Mr Fox carried them all away one snowy night. I had promised the children a dog once the chickens had died (assuming at the time our 'girls' would live for years, which they didn't); it was a surprise to my husband when the children announced, 'Mum said we could get a dog when the chickens died.' Along came Douglas and we all adore him.

Sitting out is a joy as we have bats swooping at dusk, hedgehogs hunting and hibernating, and squirrels storing nuts and then subsequently digging them up again. Mr Hoppy is a huge wild rabbit that appears and then disappears much to the annoyance of Douglas. We haven't seen 'Munching Harriet' (another wild rabbit) for some time. We had a deer jump in once, the tawny owl stops by, newts sun themselves on the warm stone, moles mess up the lawn and we have many, many pigeons... The children climb the trees to see the pigeon babies, but they're very careful to keep their distance, and they name each one. Gwen,

Billy, Lexy and Timmy were the last ones known to have fledged successfully (we hope); the sparrowhawk does an effective job in keeping the numbers down.

THE WORRY TREE

We are all fond of this tree and I'm looking at it now as I type this; it's just coming into bloom. The children climb up to their favourite branches and sit there whenever they feel inclined or need time to talk or ponder. This is a tree that they are protective of and will remember long after they have outgrown it. We call it their 'Worry Tree' and every year in late spring it becomes spectacular with big snowball-size blooms made up of tiny white individual flowers. If you shake the tree gently when in bloom the little flowers fall down like snow; it really is very pretty.

LITTLE SPARKS

Looking back I can still remember the moment that my son made me aware of his interest in natural history. He was very young (about eleven months old) and sitting in his high chair waiting for me to feed him. I sat observing his expression and stirring his food with spoon in one hand and TV remote in the other. I was searching around trying to find something for him to watch. He looked at the screen while I flicked through the channels, and eventually we stopped at a programme on birds (robins in fact) presented by Bill Oddie. I stopped flicking simply because his response on seeing the bird was immediate. He pointed at it and watched my face for a reaction; together we sat quietly watching the robins as I fed him. The programme was aimed at adults but he didn't know this of course – he just liked watching the birds.

Birds led quickly to dinosaurs and he informed me at the age of three that he wanted to be a palaeontologist. He did this by asking me what a person who looks for dinosaurs is called and I informed him that that would be a palaeontologist. He then looked at me and said, 'I want to be a palaeontologist.' I was impressed as it's a long word for a three-year-old but he pronounced it beautifully and remembered it from that moment on. We are convinced that he spent his early years imagining he was living in the Late Cretaceous period.

GRAB A NET

Our daughter, a little tired of being dinosaur prey, declared at the age of three that she wanted to be a ladybird as she's always wanted to fly (and not in a plane), and so she made herself a pair of paper wings. I had to make sure she wasn't going to jump from anything and so I followed her around outside. She went straight to the swing and her little legs got her as high as she could go. Now much older, she's still as keen on flying but has turned her attention more to those animals that can. She has always handled butterflies gently and shows great empathy if they are injured.

Our daughter collects caterpillars, moths, butterflies and 'the little bug guys'. We have a microscope that she uses to observe them; often she will flash past me with her butterfly net and then a little later I get a call to come and see what she has found. We all have a little look through the microscope and quietly marvel over her latest catch just prior to its release. Snow leopards, sloths and barn owls are also of particular interest at the moment, and in the future she hopes to help save them from extinction.

A GUEST FOR THE WINTER

I remember one day when we came home from school with a beautiful caterpillar (a privet hawk-moth) that my daughter had found. We didn't recognize what type it was at the time or know what it was going to turn into and so the children identified it in their wildlife guidebook. We tried to remember the specific spot where we had found it in order to locate the right food source; even though it was already pretty fat and appeared to be full size we still felt inclined to pop a little food in. It wasn't long before it became cocooned, buried in the soil; we then waited and waited (all winter). At first the children kept an eye on the cocoon, but eventually they stopped asking about it and naturally relied on me to inform them of any further news. When it re-emerged it was really good timing as we happened to all be in the room. I heard a faint noise coming from its enclosure and the children were able to watch as it stretched out to become a very large and beautiful moth. This amazing process was photographed by their father (who had hastily grabbed his camera). Once our fine specimen of a moth had sorted itself out and its wings were nice and dry (with a lovely dusty pink colour running through) it was ready to be released by the children, much to their delight.

THE LITTLE WASP GUYS

One impressive nature spectacle our children noted was after our daughter had collected caterpillars out in the garden, which was something she often did. She had a good number that were full size and ready for the next stage in becoming cabbage white butterflies, and we kept them safe in a net cage. One or two days later our daughter spotted tiny larvae coming out of one of the caterpillars. We watched in fascination (and a little horror) as subsequently this happened to all of them; they were dying as lots of tiny little larvae wriggled out of each of them. We needed to find out what was happening and so we did what we normally do when faced with an unknown situation: we turned to Google. Our answer was that a wasp had got to them and they had become hosts. The larvae hatched and munched their way out, killing the host caterpillars. So eight potential butterflies had turned into an army of larvae soon to become wasps. There was only one place for them...my husband, Ian, took them into work to show his colleagues, and they stayed in his office for a day or two with some managing to escape from their net enclosure, they flew straight to the windows, where (along with those remaining in the enclosure) they could easily be released.

BONJOUR, IT'S BAGUETTES

The garden playhouse became a French restaurant each summer. (They have grown out of it now: it wasn't quite the same after the sparrowhawk killed a pigeon in there, which was all terribly messy.) This was fun while it lasted, mainly because my French is so poor and they knew it. I was a rubbish waitress but the excitement and fun of having a bash at it anyway meant that they found out about France and our daughter is now keen to teach herself French (properly) as a result.

TODAY I'M GOING TO BUILD A…

…mammoth skeleton in the garden. They did this and it was impressive. It was very large, laid out beautifully on the lawn so it was impossible to mow it; you could only see what it was from a bedroom window. They build many things out of anything, but particularly cardboard boxes and sticks.

TODAY I'M GOING TO BE A…

Let's see, they have been so many animals: a tiger, raptor, sloth, elephant, polar bear and mammoth – the list is endless. They used to decide on a species together and spend the day acting, and living as that animal would, describing in detail to each other what they planned to do next or what could happen if they came across a predator, marshland or anything else they imagined. If they chose to be a species that lives in a family group then the whole family could join in and it would be enjoyable, entertaining and educational.

BASECAMP

They regularly set up a basecamp, which normally comprises a shelter built with long sticks, blankets, seating and the appropriate accessories for each season. They like to sit out in the evenings with blankets on their knees, camera set up, hot chocolate in hand to watch the bats and wait for a fly-past by the tawny owl.

FREEDOM TO SLEEP

Each summer or on a mild evening, the children have the freedom to sleep anywhere in the home or garden. They can make dens, habitats or 'nests' outside, in their bedrooms or in the study, and we put up a tent in the garden as another basecamp for the entire summer. These days, though, they both prefer sleeping in hammocks, nestled in the trees. These are all-weather hammocks and they are extremely comfortable. When the children settle in their hammocks we don't hear a peep from them until the morning. Before they settle down to sleep they do sometimes set up a camera to capture any wildlife that is creeping around.

Our son has always favoured sleeping outdoors. Some areas of the garden can look quite prehistoric at dusk, and he likes sleeping in that environment. He has a detailed plan in his mind for how to enhance the area with planting, ferns in particular – something we are going to help him with. Both children have grown up with this freedom and so it is natural and easy for them to sleep where they choose: they make a bed for the night and settle easily.

 NOTE: They do also have perfectly formed bedrooms too.

POLAR BEAR HAND

If a child has developed a close bond to nature then this can be used to enhance many situations. One good example of this is when our daughter woke up following a procedure in hospital to see her hand was bandaged. Observing her concern I reassured her and commented that her bandage did in fact look like a 'little polar bear paw'. Instantly her expression changed and she sat up to greet us; she was soon able to tuck in to some toast.

WATER, WATER EVERYWHERE

Our children both adore water and they can both swim under water. My son learnt mostly by playing in the local pool with guidance and advice from his father but also with encouragement from his class teacher during school swimming lessons.

Our daughter taught herself to swim in a week, through sheer determination to catch up with her brother and play alongside him. She did this by copying her brother and following advice from her father, who was in the pool with them. They attended every other day during this week as she was so determined to catch up.

I regularly observe their swimming and I have seen over the years how their imagination (inspired by their knowledge of nature) played a part in their learning to swim. They would often pretend to be marine or prehistoric creatures and would ask me to guess what they were as they performed the behaviour of perhaps a crocodile or a dolphin. I have seen them dive to the bottom and bob back to the surface, breaching like whales. This is only possible because of their knowledge of the natural world and it's enabled them to have hours of fun by describing and imagining what it's like to live as another species in an underwater environment.

In the past they have on occasions had baths fully clothed just out of sheer interest in what it would feel like. It's worth noting that when children have these 'I wonder what it would be like'-type thoughts it is worth saying yes, as it can sometimes become a habit for parents to automatically say no. You need to assess any implications but generally I say yes rather than no as there doesn't seem to be any reason why they shouldn't try these things out.

LET IT RAIN

Rainy days can be a huge delight for a young child; I didn't complain about the weather to them and so they didn't complain about the weather to me. Sunny days or rainy days, we coped with being outside. There were days when it was good fun (when convenient) to let them run outside in the rain just to play. When they reached the point where they were soaked and ready to come inside they would have one last splash, roll or lie in the puddles before coming in. The habit of coming back in for a warm bath followed by a cup of hot chocolate formed quickly.

 NOTE: These days they do complain a little if we have a string of rainy days, and no longer feel inclined to rush out in the rain. But they do still rush outside in a hail or snow storm and the dog follows.

'EPIC' TIMES

Explore

I've been fortunate enough to be around for many first experiences. My son took some of his first steps outdoors and I remember the first time he walked barefoot on grass; it was when he was around eleven months old. We were in the local park when another child's ball rolled towards him and he seemed eager to chase it, so I helped him to his feet. He tottered off the blanket after the ball but immediately stopped and looked down as it was the first time his bare feet had walked on grass. He came straight back to me on the blanket. I took my shoes off while reassuring him and holding his hand, and we then walked back onto the grass together.

When it came to our daughter, being the younger sibling she would naturally follow her brother and explore alongside him. She soon became determined to be independent and would want to explore and point things out to him. Both children have always been keen to come up with their own ideas and suggestions. They explore well together, fuelling each other's imagination, and you hear lots of 'Yes, but what if there was...' and 'Let's pretend there's one over there' types of animal adventures and role-play games. They would also carefully consider and select toy animals and dinosaurs to explore with and these toys would be in peril for one or two days as the game and story evolved. They would often carry on games the following day but more often than not it was the first day when the game was fresh that it was most exciting, and together they would enthusiastically muster up some great ideas. On many occasions they found themselves distracted by wildlife and this could add fun and unpredictability to their play.

Ponder

My children have the Worry Tree to sit in and mull things over, or they will walk around outside pondering things; they always find something curious to think about. My son will often sit on the grass or dusty gravel, sifting through the grass or stones, throwing things, piling them up or burying them, and he still needs to be reminded (by me) not to absent-mindedly strip the leaves off the plants as he shares his thoughts. He normally replies with, 'Sorry Mum, but I was just thinking...what if...?' and we go from there. Both children quietly observe as they ponder and wonder. Taking this time to observe in the natural world gives them valuable time to think through and create fresh ideas of what to do next.

Imagine

The joy that comes from having the time to imagine can be clearly observed when children are allowed to explore and play uninhibited. Nature, siblings, friends, books and now technology can all help to fuel their imaginations. My own children had their 'What shall we be? I know... I'm going to be a raptor or sloth' type of days. Or perhaps they would be inspired by something they'd seen and want to re-enact it. They often used to have 'animal battles' with their soft toy animals; on 'Viking day' I witnessed the soft toy version of the Battle of Maldon where one Viking (Paul the polar bear) won the battle on the back of a unicorn hand puppet while his opponent (Cyril the squirrel) was left clinging hopelessly to the back of his trusty steed which happened to be a bright pink bird of paradise. Together they share many nature-related toys and these dominate their imaginative play indoors and outdoors. When they were younger they pretended to be many different types of animal: each morning they would wake up and choose an animal to be. They still do this to some extent, except now they create animal sets with Lego or on Minecraft. They do have other toys and interests but their play has always been centred around their understanding of nature or natural events they've seen.

Create

This is where we see the outcome of their 'imagination'; in fact this is where we see the evidence of their EPIC education when it comes to how and what they create daily. Our son creates (and re-creates) what he imagines, hears about or sees physically. Sitting down at a school desk and writing is not how he likes to learn: he gains knowledge by being hands-on. Our daughter is becoming more focused to work independently and has become an avid writer and illustrates her stories, but she also likes working alongside her brother creating worlds and games with Lego or on Minecraft. Occasionally she will assist her brother in creating a new game on Blender (animation software), as they both enjoy the creative process in making the game and the build-up to playing it.

Our daughter recently decorated a cake for her toy sloths to celebrate International Sloth Day, which is held each October. They look forward to noted events like this and will create their own games for them. Other events include the WWF's Earth Hour each March (when we turn the electricity off for an hour), for which they plan family board games. They have this urge to create quite often, and amazing things happen: our son can be seen animating dinosaurs he has brought to life in Blender, and our daughter can produce a five-thousand-word story. Both children can have these intense creative days where they concentrate and focus on getting their subjects right; other days they may want to read or just generally observe and discuss random subjects as they arise.

I'm going to be brave and mention here the joys of Minecraft – oh yes, bear with me – as there are indeed many benefits. I used to be wary but not any longer. They both currently enjoy creating worlds together in Minecraft based on their knowledge of the natural world. I was a little apprehensive about this at first as I think many parents fear excessive use of online games, but having reminded myself to be mindful I'm glad I did as I can now see many benefits. The knowledge they gain from understanding their natural world is being created in front of me; they enjoy building and bringing to life all that they experience and learn about. They create knowledge-filled lands from the Earth's time line and I have sometimes been shown around these Minecraft worlds as a little character sitting in a cart; not just a mine cart either – a 'time cart' – no less, which can trundle or hurtle along the track. They even take into consideration the temperature of each time period, offering to speed up the cart's journey through the frozen eras of our Earth's history to prevent the occupants in the 'time' cart getting too chilly.

They build what they know or what they would like to find out about, knowing that if they get stuck they can research it, usually via me, technology, their friends or books. The 'What on Earth?' wall books by Christopher Lloyd[1] are particularly great for this: they can simply unfold a book which can be laid out on the floor to view in its entirety, enabling them to identify particular areas of interest.

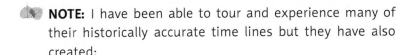 **NOTE:** I have been able to tour and experience many of their historically accurate time lines but they have also created:

- RMS *Titanic*: they built this from memory after seeing detailed images of the ship and discovering its history online. It was complete with working engines.

---

1   See www.whatonearthbooks.com

- A geological time line, following a visit to the British Geological Survey (BGS), and information obtained from their website.[2]

- A game reserve in Africa, a rather magnificent castle and a town with many houses (their residential dwellings always include authentic furnishings and subtle lighting in each room, and they ensure they accurately detail what they are describing and thinking).

- A Minecraft version of the Amazon rainforest. This was their own design based on knowledge gained over the years.

- A sloth sanctuary based on the sanctuary in Costa Rica.

- 'Life on Mars', which included a red landscape and a village constructed under a glass dome awaiting the arrival of human inhabitants, following a television programme presented by Professor Brian Cox.

- Jurassic Park and more recently Jurassic World; dinosaur parks were an obvious choice.

- A school, a holiday complex and a prison (they play this with friends and decide the rules).

- A home school, where home education is combined with a school building. They built this with old school friends to share their learning environments and take it in turns to give lectures on their favourite subjects.

---

2   The headquarters of the BGS is based at the Environmental Science Centre in Nottingham; they also have a very informative website: www.bgs.ac.uk

- A city based on Dubai (they Googled images of this city for inspiration).

- The Battle of Bosworth, following the reinterment of King Richard III in Leicester.

They have created many worlds with their friends that they 'live' in. They barter (with sheep), buy and sell houses to each other, make rules, break rules and just recently they even elected a prime minister.

As time goes by I find that I am now asking them, 'How did you know that?', 'I didn't know that' or 'Is that really what happens?', and they will tell me where they researched it, read it, watched it or heard about it. Living rurally means they can't just choose to walk over to their friends each evening and so, when it suits, they pop on their headsets and join friends playing online. This has become a beneficial way to keep in touch and develop their play.

DISTRACTION: My children are currently playing online in Minecraft with two of their old school friends. They have built two villages at the foot of two medieval castles. They have created two clans but there can only be one king... They are competing to decide who will be king and it appears the aim is to stay king for as long as you can. I have heard promises being made whenever one of them gets called away to have their tea and they have to leave their castles unguarded. They have put considerable detail into their villages. So far I have seen horses, carts, stables, windmills, a blacksmith and a bakery. They are now designing coats of arms for the castle walls; it looks a great place to be.

From this, I can see they have an understanding of history and their natural world which they can now share and enjoy with their friends. By introducing the natural world before technology I have been able to observe how this knowledge can enhance a game or even how a game can enhance their knowledge. It's a balance that works as we see how modern technology can bring their imagination to life and fuel their creativity; it also helps to keep them in touch with their friends.

Our children need little encouragement to spend as much time as possible doing the interesting things that fascinate them. The natural world is their classroom and if they ever do run out of ideas looking down on the ground, exploring the world or searching under the sea then they know they can look up. There's a fascinating sky and the splendours of the universe above them.

They are free to concentrate on the things they find interesting by giving themselves as much or as little time needed in order to retain knowledge. Childhood is their uninhibited time to be free and to learn without adult demand or peer-group pressure. It's a time to be themselves and appreciate the company of their family and friends as they explore and socialize in the world they are part of.

From an early age my children developed the habit of thinking themselves out of being bored by finding something to do. I think that a bored mind is the result of an unfulfilled one; developing the habit of being mindful and self-educating can ensure the mind is not left waiting to be entertained. This is perhaps more difficult to achieve in a controlled school environment where, if the work is too easy a child is left waiting, if the work is difficult too the child's mind switches off, or the task is just not considered interesting or relevant to the child at all. Their curiosity and their interests lead them to discover more and they have many exciting paths to explore further; with so many resources and opportunities available they have already identified courses online that may be of interest in the future. So they are both looking forward to that time of more intense study in the areas they enjoy. They currently plan to take the International General Certificate of Secondary Education (IGCSE) examinations but if they do decide to go down a more maverick route and select a more hands-on approach then we would of course support this. For now they are learning through what they choose to do.

For our son, his extensive knowledge of prehistory is expanding and he is currently enhancing this by teaching himself 3D computer animation using the Blender software. He continues to work this out for himself, seeking guidance from online support or tutorials. This computer software enables him to bring dinosaurs back to life on the screen. He studies the dinosaurs in detail away from the computer, then uses the information to set about accurately creating and animating them, concentrating on their movement and actions. His interest in creating special effects to enhance his work is also growing. He continues to amaze us with his progress; recently he has been working on a short animation film that he hopes to enter into a competition.

For our daughter it's all about animal behaviour and being creative. Whether she's drawing, playing music or writing, she's always looking to perfect her work and will often ask me how to spell things as she writes. She has a strong interest in the environment and the weather. She enjoys music and plays her cello (affectionately known as Iris) daily. She has become fascinated by sloth behaviour and because of this there has been much talk of Costa Rica and rainforests, which are sloth territory.

NOTE: They are looking forward to planning, designing and creating their own gardens within our garden, and I predict that this will be the start of a new era for them. They will be creating environments of their own to further entice wildlife. We will be helping our son to bring his ambitious plan of creating a prehistoric wildlife pond to fruition: this will be our next big family project. Work has already commenced on our daughter's design for a wildlife-friendly flower patch incorporating a series of formal, small, raised flowerbeds, which will be individually named after each of our late hens.

They both know what they have to do to achieve their future dreams and they are keen to expand their knowledge to enhance their chance of success. Currently it's a child-led (but nature- and parent-fed) education that suits their needs, with opportunities along the way to meet like-minded friends. They have grown up valuing the friendships they have made and understand they have a role in society as well as a place in the natural world. They also value their education and they know what they have to do to enhance their knowledge and gain relevant qualifications in their areas of interest, and I think they are on the right path to do so.

And a garden is a grand teacher. It teaches patience
and careful watchfulness; it teaches industry and
thrift; above all, it teaches entire trust.

Gertrude Jekyll (1899)

Chapter Eleven

AN ENVIRONMENT TO LEARN

We seem to accept that if a child performs well in a school environment and strives to reach the targets set for them, then there is little doubt that the school environment is teaching them all they need in order to succeed in the modern world today. Society doesn't appear to consider, recognize or accept any other learning environment on offer to its children than the mainstream school system. When the time comes most parents will choose the school that they consider most suitable. Some may place total trust in the school and choose not to be too involved with their children's education; others will strive to govern the school; and many parents will spend time discussing the teaching staff and their methods as they go about sharing information about the school, often commenting on their child's progress with other parents.

Through observations of my children in their school environment it became obvious (to me) that some types of mind, particularly creative minds, do not always fare quite so well in a target-driven environment. But I came across a number of parents who appeared to be going to great lengths and working with the school to ensure that their children (creative or not) conformed.

I would ask the question – what if schools were to prioritize singing? How many of us would feel comfortable enough to stand up and sing in tune? I've never been able to sing in tune so what would happen if the school insisted and expected me to do so? I would be keen to please and so would probably suggest I could perhaps draw for them instead, as I'm pretty good at drawing and I enjoy it, but they would no doubt suggest I keep trying to sing, as this may be more beneficial to me in the long term.

Perhaps I would then be offered a place in a special group where I could sing out of tune with others just like me and even miss out on other lessons in order to obtain better singing results; but what if that caused me to dread school and become anxious? What if gaining knowledge was no longer enjoyable?

Any joy that I may have gained from learning to sing would be lost. Reluctance would soon replace enthusiasm when it came to me trying to sing in order to gain their approval. What if my parents were also showing concern that I wasn't going to be able to sing, and brought it up in the home environment? Realization would sink in that I had to work twice as hard in a subject that actually holds very little or absolutely no interest for me. Eventually, if I did manage to reach the expectations of modern society, then I could still feel that I had failed by missing out on the opportunity to discover just how good I could have been at drawing.

This is similar to what is happening in our schools today with the current target-driven emphasis on mathematics and literacy, and as a result many creative, interesting and curious minds are having to conform to fit into a system that will leave them unfulfilled and unchallenged as their own interests take a backseat. Any knowledge happily gained and retained through curiosity prior to starting school is downgraded, interests become a recreational pastime and only school work is considered a priority – and this comes at them in the (dare I say) rather dull form of the current state curriculum.

To add further to the blow, many can only observe as those more suited to the environment become recognized by their teaching professionals as 'gifted and talented' (as opposed to what?), often being rewarded with special privileges. The race to be successful appears to have become more important than the knowledge that a child actually gains and retains. Children are acutely mindful of their peers' targets and placement when it comes to ability groups; pressure is being applied from all directions in today's classroom.

I can therefore think of many more inspirational environments to be in than an underfunded pre-fabricated school classroom, packed with children with only one teacher (and possibly an assistant), and given an hour or so in which to settle down and do something creative. If we hope to encourage creative thinking in future generations then we will need to allow creative teaching in schools.

We are all individuals with value and interests, and as a society we simply need to acknowledge the fact that some children enjoy learning naturally in a calm environment while others enjoy the more structured approach of a put-together curriculum. It is down to the child and the parent to decide the best environment in which the child can gain knowledge.

As parents we need to ensure that our own children appreciate and understand the relevance of all types of interests and subsequently the knowledge gained from those interests. We should all know and respect the fact that there are different styles when it comes to teaching. It is the responsibility of a parent to ensure their child is educated and therefore most would like to assume their child feels valued and respected in their chosen learning establishment.

A child will naturally look to a parent for guidance when it comes to learning; in return a parent should show that they have the confidence to respond naturally without doubt or the need to consult others. No parent should ever feel they have to justify what is best for their child when it comes to how they gain and retain valuable knowledge. Children are capable of discovering the specific learning environment that suits them best.

As touched upon earlier in the book, I think that as a society we all have to learn to respect each other's decisions, accept all educational choices and trust that all parents will endeavour to provide and do what is in the best interest for their own children;

it is, after all, their responsibility to do so. No home-educating family should feel they have to justify their child's education.

For my children, who had already experienced an EPIC childhood in their earlier years, the reason to stay in school would always come down to friendships: these were strong and their only reason to stay in school. But also, at first, they didn't think that parents were equipped to educate their children and so the 'No offence, Mum, but you would be rubbish' hurdle had to be overcome. This turned out to be of particular importance as it dawned on me that the moment I sent them to school I had ranked parenting lower than teaching – something my children now understand not to be the case.

DISTRACTION: As I write this my son is designing a zoo. He is currently reading *The Aye-Aye and I* by Gerald Durrell and true to form he will now design and build what he has read about the night before. My daughter is beside me typing on her laptop. Douglas (our young Border terrier) is asleep in his brand-new dog bed and he currently has our full attention as just a moment ago he started to whimper in his sleep. The children instantly stopped what they were doing, and as we all watched him, he twitched a little and whimpered some more. We all found this amusing and then my daughter said, 'Proof, then, that he dreams.'

I would assume so, but it would be interesting to know for sure: one for her to research later.

The way my own children behave is often predictable. Our daughter will often wonder 'What is it like if...' and talk her thoughts and ideas through; she explores and ponders quietly. She has been described by others as diligent, humble and wise. Our son is gentle in nature but more inclined to wonder 'What will happen if I do this...' and so his approach is sometimes easier to observe. His sister is therefore also learning from his actions or, perhaps more to the point, from the consequences of his actions.

Here are a few of the lessons they have learnt from playing outside in their natural environment over the years: If you leave small toys on the driveway they may be destroyed. If you build a den on the driveway it will eventually have to be moved. If you climb high up into the trees wearing wellington boots you may get stuck. If you fall into water fully clothed and wearing your wellington boots then you will be deemed lucky to be alive and feel a little uncomfortable afterwards. If you 'rescue' a tree from felling in the garden and choose to replant it outside your bedroom window then it may grow to be very tall. If your mother drives off one day with your treasured allosaurus dinosaur toy on the roof of her car (but fails to return with it) then you must try to put it behind you and forgive her...dinosaurs do roam. If you swing on tree branches, you may find (as years go by) that they may no longer be as strong as you think; if you then 'fix' snapped tree branches with rope they will eventually 'wilt' and parents do notice. If you fill the freezer with tubs of water containing 'ice-age mammals', make sure you choose a good time to bash them out again. If you decide to move gravel from the driveway in your tractor-trailer then you may discover that it's not a particularly good idea to empty it out onto the grass. If your father subsequently mows that lawn (with the delight of hidden gravel) then as you now know gravel can fly like a bullet and break windows. If you dive into the borders then plants will be broken and damaged. If you dig out dinosaur nests (even though they do look amazing) make sure they are clearly marked and not dug out in front of any entrance that leads into the house. If you switch on a little battery-powered car and place it on top of your head it will get caught up in your hair; if your little sister then copies your actions the result will be the same and you will both require a 'car removal hair cut'. If you bury toys please be aware that you may not always remember where they are. If you dive into ditches make sure you have appropriate clothing (i.e. not your best clothes). If you get stuck in the mud don't call for your grandma to go in after you – she's always keen to help but she'll only get stuck in the mud herself. Finally, any dinosaur that finds its way down the toilet can't (under any circumstances) be returned to the toy box.

I think it's obvious that we have a home where children play freely and wildlife is very welcome, so much so that it sometimes finds its way in independently (we had a little robin in the kitchen yesterday), or otherwise it comes in attached to the children; either way it gets observed (currently there is a little shield bug waiting to be viewed under the microscope; he's fine – we'll release him later). Every season we meet new 'wild' guests that are all welcome as they add to the sense of adventure and interest.

At home our children each have a 'base' where they can study. They sit next to a window, which they can open for fresh air without asking; they can listen to the birds singing as they learn. They take breaks when needed and play outside in the garden when they choose. In a school environment children are encouraged to sit down quietly (often on the floor with their legs crossed) and have to put their hand up if they want to speak. As adults I'm sure we wouldn't tolerate sitting on the floor for long and yet it doesn't occur to us to question it on behalf of our children.

At the school our children attended they were allocated a new place to sit each term and therefore after each holiday they did not know where they would be placed or whom they would be sitting with, as the teacher chose for them. This caused considerable anxiety as they both had a small group of like-minded friends that they were comfortable with and there were others with whom they absolutely did not want to be placed. So returning to school was always an anxious time. Once again I ask if this would be tolerated in an adult working environment – would we welcome our place being moved without our consent or denied the chance to voice an opinion?

With their home education our children can decide if they need a break or not. Sometimes they just prefer to get stuck into something interesting and will only stop for a snack or for lunch, depending on what they are doing. I have found that they are also now taking the time to discuss and plan their day a little more. They normally check what the other has planned and find out what the weather is going to be like: they Google the weather each morning. They normally ask what they are having for lunch and what time it will be, and plan the day around their meal; they are very capable and organized.

They have clocks on their desks and we have two other clocks downstairs. The one in the sitting room no longer has hands (so it's useless) but it was such an attractive clock and I wished to keep it so I simply wrote 'Oh my goodness! Where has the time gone?' across its very pretty face, so it's become a piece of 'art', or perhaps more of a curiosity. We do, however, have a fully functioning kitchen wall clock that they are encouraged to use as they do time themselves with some tasks. If you ask them the time they normally will have a rough idea of what it is, and occasionally they still prefer to guess rather than walk to have a look.

TALK, TALK AND THEN TALK SOME MORE…

Children like to explore, ask questions and talk. At home we do lots of walking and talking, eating and talking, cooking and talking, gardening and talking. We talk about subjects so diverse…

Initially we all kept home education journals (most de-schooling home educators start out doing this; it seems to be a natural thing to do) and we tried to keep them updated. I used to write down their questions and some of our conversations but as time has gone on we find that talking just rolls into the evenings. I believe talking freely to each other this way helps to build respect between parent and child. I also feel that this respect can lead to natural development of a child's maturity.

Here are just some of their early home education questions:

- Can smoke burn?

- When were diving boards invented?

- Can shadows be in colour?

121

- Do cows walk in straight lines?
- Can you really be hypnotized?
- Is the moon moving?
- When is it OK to tell a lie?
- What is a flash fire?
- Can you be born with no sense of smell?
- How did Charles Darwin die?
- What's a rip current?
- Does the Queen own all the swans?
- When can I have a leopard gecko?
- Why are people vegetarian?
- Why is it called an Indian summer?
- When is the next eclipse?
- What's a ceasefire baby?
- What is a basement for?
- What is magnetism?
- Can you drink tea without milk?
- Where do wild pigs live and are they omnivores?
- Does the Queen have a surname?
- Why does every label say 'Made in China'?
- What are our bones made of?
- Does Douglas think he is a human?
- Why doesn't snow settle on wet ground?
- Why are cartoon scientists always wearing glasses?

- What is colour?

- How long can you live without food?

- What would happen if the world stopped spinning?

- Do dogs think like us?

- Do birds see in colour?

- What does the prime minister do?

- Is there a question that Google can't answer?

- Do animals have the same type of blood as we do?

- How long is the flight to Costa Rica?

- If some flowers are poisonous why is it safe to eat honey?

- How does your memory work?

- Are dogs ticklish?

- What does vitamin B12 do?

- If you dug a hole through the centre of the world and right the way through to the other side, would you be able to fall all the way down it or would you have to climb out the other end?

NOTE: Our son asked this last question when he was curious about gravity. Finding the answer involved the whole family and we enjoyed coming up with a number of scenarios and discussed the implications of how gravity could potentially pull, stop or slow you down.

The questioning never stops: every day they ask questions. We all know that children will naturally ask a vast amount of questions if they have the opportunity to do so. It's been made obvious to me that if children are given the chance to talk freely then they are naturally curious and will seek to find explanations and share their own knowledge, ideas and thoughts. We shouldn't underestimate this questioning; if we give a child the impression they don't need to ask questions because they will be told everything they need to know at school then this habit will stick, and they will wait to be told information rather than naturally search for it.

Children need to feel that they can talk freely and have their own theories of how or why things happen; their interactions and thoughts have a value and this should be acknowledged by their parents and role models. If their theories don't turn out to be right they can join in, discuss and think again. This is perhaps more easily achieved at home as getting things wrong in a school environment can cause embarrassment to a child and trigger unnecessary comments from peers. They need to know the importance of making mistakes and that it's not always possible to get things right first time.

For both of my children, who naturally talk things through, the 'hands up if you know the right answer' approach at school became detrimental to their learning, particularly in mathematics, and as a result some confidence building has been required at home in this area.

I have heard many parents casually comment that their children don't really feel inclined to talk to them much about school. When my own children went to school I noticed that they seemed to prefer talking to me about their friendships rather than the content of their lessons. To address this, I believe it would be worthwhile for schools to prioritize children's common interest in nature, which may naturally result in more talking amongst peers, parents and teachers. Children would soon see that their most beneficial 'subject' isn't just associated with school and this would become even more apparent as they developed a habit to recognize the value and importance of what naturally surrounds them in all environments daily.

For now, there are in fact two questions that you could ask your children that may help to get them talking about their day in school: 'What was the best bit of your day?' followed by 'What was the worst bit of your day?' This works really well if you share the 'best and worst bits' of your own day with them.

NOTE: It helps considerably, of course, if you don't have a mobile phone in your hand when you collect or greet your children after school, as they will naturally be hoping to be the focus of your attention.

It probably helps that my own children have seen that I have managed to lose all three mobile phones that I have owned over the years. Being at the end of a phone seems a little like a burden to me and so it is kept (when found) in the car for emergencies only. My children don't currently have mobile phones but I'm sure they will one day. Ian does have a phone as this is required for his work, and the children see him using it regularly (they also play games on it when it's left lying around), so we are not against them by any means – they just aren't always appropriate to have around.

There is another consideration that we are able to address at home in their learning environment, and that is how we learn and store historical events. We focus on time lines, lots of them: this way our children can build an accurate account of when things occurred in our history and in what order. They can then see for themselves what was happening across the world and identify the period in other communities and cultures to build a comprehensive idea of world events. This helps them to build a clearer understanding of all environments.

In contrast, topics in schools are delivered within a short timescale, a burst of information covered in a disjointed fashion: the Second World War, the Vikings, the Tudors, for example. This style of teaching rarely allows a child to consider or relate timescales to the bigger picture around them or connect any significance to when these events actually happened in relation to what else may have been going on at the same time in the world.

During my children's later years at school the continuous push to achieve good results meant that they were repeatedly tested and timed in order to give fast and accurate answers. The children were judging and taking notice of each other's work simply because the teachers were emphasizing it by comparing and placing the children in ability groups. The school continued to focus on achieving targets and following a set structure rather than creating an environment where learning became the natural outcome inspired by creative teaching.

READ, READ AND THEN READ SOME MORE...

At home and at school, reading is encouraged. As a family we read a great deal; we find it doesn't matter what format we read in – it's always useful. I can often be found in bookshops, sniffing and admiring the books, and as a result our children see bookshops as a familiar environment to explore regularly.

Reading out loud at home

As well as talking a lot, our children also like to read a lot. They read to themselves and occasionally out loud. We used to all have a go at reading out loud, either by writing a story or choosing one to read out loud, ensuring we put plenty of fun and expression into it.

Reading out loud in school

At school both of our children used to like reading to their class teacher and the comments in their reading diaries were good. However, my husband and I noticed that when they occasionally had to read with somebody else, such as a parent or a teaching assistant, they would sometimes have the odd comment along the lines of 'more expression needed'. Over time I got to know the initials of those signing the book and looked a little further into the personalities involved. It soon became obvious what was happening: the children were relaxed, happy and confident reading to their familiar teacher but when asked to read with anyone who, let's just say, didn't always smile or have a friendly manner, then they felt awkward and uncomfortable. This is understandable, as I know I would have felt the same in their shoes.

We all know that books are good for children. If they read at home, in libraries, in schools – if they read books anywhere – it will enhance their world. It helps them to concentrate, think and imagine and they can be transported into new and fascinating worlds.

I have always read to our children. From the moment they were able to sit up and prior to every bedtime they would have a cuddle on my knee and we would read books (normally dinosaur or animal related). Even now we find ourselves still quoting and recounting books from their early childhood. It wasn't long before they were choosing books to read together at bedtime (still dinosaur or animal related). I would read to them and often stop to ask if they could picture the scene, what they thought of the characters and what they thought would happen next. I would encourage them to guess and we would carry on reading. They would often interrupt and pre-empt what would be coming next, we would dissect the story, and there were times when we couldn't wait to find out what was going to happen so we would read on. Now they read silently to themselves at bedtime – still mostly dinosaur- or animal-related fact or fiction, but dragons and wizards did become popular for a while.

Ian wasn't read to at home as a child and as a result he has little interest in picking up a fiction book today (although he did enjoy reading to our children when they were younger). His childhood was filled with scientific interests and his passion for photographing wildlife, and he is still drawn to factual books rather than fiction. Our children now enjoy both fact and fiction; this wasn't intentional and I believe they just observed what both of their parents were interested in reading and naturally followed their lead.

DISTRACTION: My daughter has just pointed out that we have a little wild rabbit in the garden.

LISTEN, LISTEN AND THEN LISTEN SOME MORE

As adults we assume peace and quiet can be found in the great outdoors; we like to relish the ambient calmness it has to offer and this is often how we see the natural world depicted. We can of course enjoy the calming effects of the natural world but in fairness to all other species, if we take the time to listen, we can hear that nature is anything but quiet.

In my own children's learning environment they can hear how wonderfully busy the natural world is and they have grown to appreciate that many of the species living locally have an awful lot to do and say: from the delicate sound of a wasp chewing wood to create material for its nest to the cacophony that erupts when a magpie gets too close to a pigeon's nest.

Children seem to have a natural aptitude for tuning in to their senses; my own children often pick up on a sound in nature long before I hear it. Over the years their interest in the natural world and keenness to sleep outdoors have shown them that nature is also noisy at night. The eerie sound of a distant fox call can still wake them but they now sleep through the communication between two tawny owls and the grunts and snuffles of the hedgehogs.

As infants my own children were introduced to the dawn chorus and they have grown to appreciate the 'songs' of our garden birds. The sound of birdsong enhances their learning environment and for my son this means that the connection between our garden birds and dinosaurs is never far from his mind; for my daughter, when she plays her cello with the doors open, the sounds of nature flood in as the sound of her cello spills out, enabling her (perhaps unwittingly) to join in with nature's ensemble.

MUSIC

Another interesting development for me to observe is that my children sometimes listen to music as they work. This enables them to feel inspired as they concentrate and it appears to enhance their creativity. They select the type of music in the same way any adult would select music, depending on their mood or circumstance. Lately I've been hearing the film score from *Jurassic Park* by John Williams, and music by the Piano Guys ('Beethoven's 5 Secrets' in particular).

NOTE: The quote chosen at the end of this chapter is a thought that occurred to me while walking on the Malvern Hills in Worcestershire. Before we were married, Ian drove me one morning to the hills as 'he had a plan' (a surprise day out; it was a three-hundred-mile round trip). When we got there, he led me on foot to his favourite spot. This was a familiar place to him, having lived in Malvern, and this spot and the surrounding area were ones that he would often go to photograph. However, on this particular day he simply asked me if I would like to marry him, and that very moment is now recalled and treasured perhaps more than the wedding day itself. We have since been back to 'our spot' with the children; we talked and walked with them on the hills, admiring the view as we ventured together right up to the highest peak.

With a strong bond to nature, taking in the awe and wonder of a magnificent and natural landscape enables clarity of thought and provides great comfort.

(My own observation)

Chapter Twelve

TIME FOR A LITTLE INSPIRATION

In this chapter I would like to draw a little more attention to the well-documented fact that our environment and natural world can, and has always been, a natural inspiration for many, and the evidence of this can be observed all around us. What appears to be less well documented is how the valuable knowledge gained from our natural learning environment has influenced many of those who have spent time away from the limitations of a structured school environment. You will discover from the famous figures listed in this chapter just how curiosity of the natural world became the fuel for providing answers to many questions and how this led to new and exciting discoveries.

My research and interest led me to look into the childhood history of many past lives (and there are still so many more to research) and, of course, many present ones. What I learnt confirmed my own thoughts and findings about what we can achieve by simply being educated or nurtured in our preferred natural environment and having the time and freedom for EPIC opportunities which allow us to develop our interests and work things out for ourselves. It can all start in those important years of discovery, our early childhood years.

NOTE: Mainstream school may be viewed by many as the motorway to success, but consider this: could home education be viewed as the quietly travelled coastal path to contentment? Success and/or contentment — either one could lead to the other, and I think we are capable of selecting a preference when it comes to how we would like to travel.

BEATRIX POTTER
Author, illustrator and natural scientist
28 July 1866–22 December 1943

Beatrix Potter showed at a young age that she had an artistic nature, and was frequently taken on trips to galleries by her parents. Beatrix and her brother were educated at home; it was common in those days to be cared for by a governess. Her early interest in painting and drawing was encouraged and kept her occupied during her outdoor lessons, where she would sketch plants and animals. Although Beatrix was born in London she enjoyed the countryside and family holidays to Scotland and the Lake District. These holidays had an enormous influence on her study of natural history. She became a collector of specimens and the young Beatrix would return from family holidays with an array of wildlife collected on her travels – rabbits, newts, caterpillars and others – which she would observe and care for in her schoolroom. Some of her early water-colour and pencil specimen drawings are now stored at the Victoria and Albert Museum in London. Her interest in natural history became the inspiration for her many stories.

Beatrix Potter developed a strong friendship with one governess, Annie Moore, and would write illustrated letters to her children; in these she would tell the tales of her many pets. One of these tales was to become the picture book *Peter Rabbit*. Beatrix would later use the profit made from her first six books to purchase her first farm. She died in 1943 leaving her land and farms in the capable hands of the National Trust.

GERALD DURRELL, OBE
Author and naturalist
7 January 1925–30 January 1995

Gerald Durrell's work is widely documented. He was born in India in 1925, and I found it amusing to read that the first word he spoke was 'zoo' and that he had insisted on regular visits to zoos. Gerald moved to England with his mother and siblings following the untimely death of his father. They soon tired of the British weather and the family found themselves on the move again, this time to the Greek island of Corfu. It was here that the ten-year-old Gerald thrived, spending time collecting and observing wildlife specimens in the company of his family and local islanders. He shared a fascination for wildlife with one of his tutors, Dr Theodore Stephanides, and many happy days were spent exploring the island. He would later write about his family life and experiences and his work remains popular today. My own children are currently enjoying his work.

> It is a curious thing, but when you keep animals as pets you tend to look upon them so much as miniature human beings that you generally manage to impress some of your own characteristics on to them. This anthropomorphic attitude is awfully difficult to avoid. If you possess a golden hamster and are always watching the way he sits up and eats a nut, his little pink paws trembling with excitement, his pouches bulging as he saves in his cheeks what cannot be eaten immediately, you might one day come to the conclusion that he looks exactly like your Uncle Amos sitting, full of port and nuts, in his favourite club. From that moment the damage is done. The hamster continues to behave like a hamster, but you regard him only as a miniature Uncle Amos, clad in a ginger fur-coat, forever sitting in his club, with his cheeks bulging with food. (Durrell 2012, p.131)

His legacy continues of course through his internationally recognized trust, created in 1963, the name of which was changed in 1999 to honour their founder. The Durrell Wildlife Conservation Trust continues today, and their mission remains the same: to save species from extinction.

DAME AGATHA CHRISTIE, DBE
Novelist and playwright
15 September 1890–12 January 1976

Agatha Christie is held in high regard as one of the best-selling novelists of all time; well known for her crime writing and detective novels, she also wrote the world's longest-running play, *The Mousetrap*. There have been many film and television adaptations of her work and these remain popular today. As a young child Agatha Christie was educated at home, mostly by her father, where she would also spend time playing with her animals. As an adult she commented that her childhood had been a happy one. Her mother was a storyteller and thought that her young daughter would like to consider reading by the time she was eight, but the young Agatha had other ideas and taught herself to read before that age; she became an avid reader and enjoyed reading not just children's stories and poetry but also thrillers.

J.R.R. TOLKIEN, CBE, FRSL
Writer, philologist, poet and university professor
3 January 1892–2 September 1973

I have particularly enjoyed digging a little deeper into the fascinating world of J.R.R. Tolkien. He was born in Africa, although he returned to England in his early years where his mother, Mabel Tolkien, educated her young children at home. The young J.R.R. Tolkien was a keen pupil with an interest in botany, and liked to draw plants.

Although a professor of Anglo-Saxon at Oxford University and a major scholar of the English language, to many he is known for his widely read works *The Hobbit* and *The Lord of the Rings*. In later years he would walk the Malvern Hills in Worcestershire and spend time 're-living his work' with like-minded hiking companions. They would compare this inspirational landscape (which he had been able to view as a child from his family home) to that of the White Mountains in the Middle-earth landscape that he created in his work.

NOTE: Having walked the Malverns on several occasions (including hot-footing it up there for my marriage proposal), I can see why he found them inspiring; people who encounter them often return again and again. They are ancient hills that dominate the landscape and I think this adds to their wonder.

GERTRUDE JEKYLL
Horticulturist, garden designer, artist and author
29 November 1843–8 December 1932

Being an artist, Gertrude Jekyll had an eye for colour and an early passion for understanding the beauty of the natural world. Gertrude did not become popular for her garden designs until later in life, as her main interest had initially focused on painting and embroidery. Following the deterioration of her eyesight she turned her attention to garden design.

Her passion for and knowledge of gardening developed from childhood. As a young girl she left London with her family and moved to Bramley House in Surrey. Her new home had a large garden and her memories of that time remained with her and were to become the foundation of her many achievements. A prolific gardener, her designs were widely admired and considered to be simple but effective. One of her books, *Children and Gardens*, was first published in 1908 and was written specifically with younger gardeners in mind.

IAN FLEMING
Author
28 May 1908–12 August 1964

James Bond, 007: a familiar name and one we know so well (with the actor Sir Sean Connery being 'the best Bond' I think). I discovered that the name 'James Bond' was chosen by Ian Fleming from a book he used to identify the birds around him on the island of Jamaica: *Birds of the West Indies*, written by ornithologist James Bond. Ian Fleming didn't start writing until later in life but the fact remains that he was influenced by his surroundings, and from his own admission we probably wouldn't even have 'Bond' if he hadn't been drawn to the beauty of Jamaica, where he purchased 'Goldeneye', his bungalow.

Interestingly the children who appear in the popular film version of Ian Fleming's work *Chitty Chitty Bang Bang* appear to be tutored by their father throughout. This story was written for Fleming's son, Casper, and remains a much-loved family film for many. The child characters are introduced early and can be seen playing truant from school, enjoying adventures and being told stories by their imaginative and inventive father. I think the story remains popular today as it captures the joy of imagination, close family bonds and the curiosity of childhood.

ALFRED RUSSEL WALLACE, OM, FRS
Naturalist and explorer
8 January 1823–7 November 1913

CHARLES DARWIN, FRS
Naturalist and geologist
12 February 1809–19 April 1882

These two remarkable gentlemen led very different lives and yet they were able to develop similar theories regarding 'evolution by natural selection' at the same point in history; this is quite extraordinary, especially if you then consider that they each had their own independent approach and came from entirely different educational backgrounds. They did, however, share a common interest: they both had an early fascination for the natural world and they each had a curiosity about beetles.

NOTE: My own children have shown great interest in the lives and work of these two men, and as a family we regularly visit museums in Cambridge and London to research and find out more. The Natural History Museum in London holds a vast collection of their written work, specimens and other items from their travels.

Having unlimited access to the NHM website is also a great way for my children (and myself) to access information digitally. They often take a look at the information and collections available online and search the site out of curiosity.

THOMAS HENRY HUXLEY, PC, FRS, FLS
Biologist and anatomist
4 May 1825–29 June 1895

The Huxley name is noted for being a family that excelled in many fields. Along with Thomas Huxley we also widely acknowledge the work of other family members, including Aldous Huxley (writer, novelist) and his brother Sir Julian Huxley (biologist); the latter went on to be one of the founders of the World Wildlife Fund (now known simply as WWF) along with (amongst others) Sir Peter Scott.

Thomas Huxley was born in London. His father was a maths teacher but the family fell on hard times and so the young Thomas left formal education at the age of ten, after only two years of study. His intelligence and curiosity were noted as a boy, and despite only spending two years in school he was determined to self-educate himself – and did just that in a number of subjects, including science, German, history and philosophy. He began to favour Darwin's theory of evolution and would become known in his field as 'Darwin's Bulldog'.

Thomas Huxley was respected as a biologist and became recognized for his modern approach to educating students, encouraging them to learn through practical experiments rather than concentrating on textbooks.

SIR PETER SCOTT
Conservationist and artist
14 September 1909–29 August 1989

Scott was an influential conservationist and this was recognized when he received a knighthood for his contribution in 1973, the first of its kind for conservation. He was also a naturalist, ornithologist, broadcaster, sportsman and the founding chairman of WWF.

Peter Scott was the son of the Antarctic explorer Robert Falcon Scott, although sadly he was probably too young to remember much about his father, who died in 1912 on his second Antarctic expedition. It is well known that Peter's father wrote (in his last letter home) a sentence that may have contributed to his son's passion for wildlife: he asked his wife whether she could encourage him to have an interest in natural history.[1]

MARY ANNING
Palaeontologist and collector of fossils
21 May 1799–9 March 1847

Mary Anning is a name my children recognize, having viewed some of the items she collected; the Sedgwick Museum of Earth Sciences in Cambridge have the ichthyosaur she discovered on display. She was born into a humble family and they lived on the Jurassic Coast at Lyme Regis in Dorset. Mary had very little education but despite this she taught herself to be literate and

---

1   The Polar Museum, Scott Polar Research Institute, Cambridge, is a great place to visit; they also have a very informative website: www.spri.cam.ac.uk

studied geology and anatomy. Her work became recognized and she was acknowledged as an expert in her field – the study of fossils – and held in such high regard by eminent scientists that they would journey to visit her.

Mary's father used to take his children to the beach to collect fossils and sell them to visitors; her entire life was spent in the area around Lyme Regis. Later, as a scientist, she was considered to be a celebrity but still chose to spend her time collecting fossils. My own children like the idea that she used to go fossil hunting with her dog, Tray. Mary Anning also made the discovery that ink from squid-like belemnites can be ground up and used for drawing.

This extraordinary collection of minds will, I hope, inspire, as we can acknowledge from these past lives that children can be educated in many environments and surroundings, and that as a modern-day society we need to accept and act on the fact that we cannot continue to underestimate children when it comes to how they like to learn. We have to consider the needs of each child and observe how the natural world could provide them all with a strong foundation for their future interests and study.

Having covered past lives, let us return to the present and have a quick look at two highly regarded and inspirational figures who are part of my own children's world today.

CRESSIDA COWELL
Author
Born 15 April 1966

As a family we have been enjoying the 'How to Train Your Dragon' series by Cressida Cowell. In each of her books she tells of how her experiences as a child on a secluded Scottish island, rich in Viking history, sparked her imagination. She would spend time isolated on the island, surrounded by nature and in the company of her family, where she would play, explore and write. This influenced her thoughts, inspiring her to create the amazing world of Berk and the much-loved Hiccup and Astrid, whose adventures are read by my own children.

The natural history Cressida Cowell encountered as a child played a part in the creation of the many species of dragons that she describes so beautifully in her books. The insight she gained from observing the many sea creatures she encountered on fishing trips enabled her to imagine and create spectacular new species for our children to enjoy.

> Look around you at your own world now. You may not see dragons, but notice the numberless quantities of species that we have in our woods, in the air, in the mountains, in the skies. The proud lion, the mighty elephant, the seals, the birds, the thousands of types of beetle. One of those beetles could be the cure for some terrible disease…
>
> Take care, dear reader, that we are looking after the boundless wonder of our world. (Cowell 2014, Preface)

I felt encouraged when I read this passage. It was a clear and inspiring message to her readers and a great way to reach them; this message also remained on my own mind.

SIR DAVID ATTENBOROUGH
Broadcaster and naturalist
Born 8 May 1926

Sir David Attenborough is a broadcaster with worldwide appeal who can reach all generations with his enthusiasm for our natural world. He has a fascination for natural history that has been obvious since childhood and remains with him today. As a family we continue to enjoy his wildlife documentaries and tend to watch them more than once.

> People sometimes ask me when and how I first got interested in animals. I have to admit that seems to me an extraordinary question. I find it hard to believe that any normal child is born without any interest. I recall taking a five-year-old for a walk

in a Devon meadow. He turned over a stone. 'Look,' he said, 'a slug. What a little treasure!' And quite right too. The way it moved, sliding along without the help of legs. Those eyes on the end of a couple of waving stalks that retracted when he touched them. Astonishing! (Attenborough 2009, p.7)

NOTE: I have just mentioned Sir David Attenborough to my children, and my son commented that they had recently been speaking of him to their friend while playing on Minecraft. They were building in their tundra region when the friend asked what 'the tundra' was. My son described the cold landscape and the conditions that caused the sparseness of the trees, repeating what he had seen and heard on one of Attenborough's documentaries. Their friend now understands this and has mentioned it since.

Families can also be inspiring and my own is no exception. I consider my husband to be a wonderfully calm influence in our world with his quick wit and dry sense of humour. He thinks and he ponders, he makes us laugh and he takes great interest in how his children like to learn, inspiring them with his own interests. When the children spend time with him in the evenings and at the weekends they have their enthusiasm fed, although his interest in 'quantum entanglement' is something that they may have to think more about later on in their journey, should they feel inclined to do so.

NOTE: I sometimes find myself really trying to understand quantum entanglement. It takes some thinking about but I wonder if it could eventually be linked to the chemistry that enables us to bond to each other and nature? Somehow the entanglement theory seems appropriate when we think along these lines; Ian will continue to mull it over. With so many new discoveries we consider ourselves very fortunate to be living in these inspiring (and curious) times.

My husband's interests have always included nature, science and photography. These have been lifelong and encouraged by his father and grandparents; his extensive knowledge of human biology comes from his mother, who fulfilled her childhood dream of becoming a nurse. In her youth she used to draw detailed sketches of the human bone structure. Always a keen gardener and writer of poems, she can now focus on these interests in her retirement.

NOTE: My daughter has just received a beautiful letter from her grandmother. It arrived in time for her birthday and included a selection of magazine cuttings about butterflies. Letters are very special to receive and this was of course shown in my daughter's expression on opening the envelope.

My husband often recounts stories from his own childhood and he remembers his first attempt at photography, which was to try to photograph a swift in flight (he was quite ambitious). His attempts were unsuccessful, so – undeterred – he turned his focus to wildlife that remained stationary for at least a few moments, such as dragonflies and frogs. He also recounts stories of his father's travels and adventures around the world (through his work), and these are inspirational as well as educational for our children.

His mother wasn't (and still isn't) a pet person and so when she finally agreed that he could keep a terrapin you can imagine his delight as a boy. He chose well: in fact the 'terrapin' he picked, because it looked a little different to the others, looked this way for a good reason. He soon discovered that 'Arnold the Terrapin' was in fact a very young Chinese softshell turtle that could stretch his neck and snap rather aggressively for food (and fingers!). Further research led to the startling discovery that Arnold would eventually grow to be the size of a dinner plate. Needless to say the wonderful Arnold soon found himself travelling to a new home at the local zoo. Feeling slightly disappointed, Ian turned his attention to Tarquin, a kissing gourami fish. I even got to meet this little fish myself as he lived for many years.

Once again we see how spending time with adults and hearing about older generations can give children the chance to be inspired as they gain valuable knowledge through hearing and discussing recollections. This helps to build strong family bonds and connections that develop their sense of belonging and security. Over time this sense of belonging (I believe) will enable them to venture out and travel further afield in the world, with a quiet confidence.

DISTRACTION: I'm getting a scent of spring from the garden; it's wafting in as I type. There's a subtle breeze today with only a little touch of a chill. Each season our garden and home have an array of scents. We have a rather rampant jasmine that is now far too heavy for the pergola, and another plant that is known simply as our 'not jasmine': it's a shrub that looks and smells like jasmine but isn't... I really must look it up.

> *The good thing about home school is that you're*
> *allowed to play on the grass when it's wet.*
>
> (My daughter's observation)

Chapter Thirteen

PLAY AND FRIENDSHIPS

Most parents embarking on the journey of home education will have already taken into account the value of friendships and naturally considered how their children will socialize. In this chapter I will be looking closely at how children are able to develop socially within their chosen learning environments.

It's important to say that, as a family, we have not found a need to succumb to the often-unhelpful advice (so readily given) from the many curious minds that struggle to come to terms with the idea that home education can be considered a viable alternative to school simply because of their own interpretation of how children should socialize.

There appears to be an assumption in modern society that children need to develop coping strategies at an early age and build friendships within a large population of children. But school is not a natural environment for any young child, and so recognizing that it could have limitations when it comes to developing a mature understanding of how to socialize in the world our children live in meant this wasn't a major worry or consideration for us.

Having spent time watching my children learn through their play, particularly when it was uninterrupted, I became aware of their need to have unrestricted amounts of time to talk and play freely, whether it's just the two of them, with me, with one or two friends or within a larger group of friends. They thrive on the opportunity to take all the time they need to invent, create and develop the games they would like to play.

Some would say school is the ideal place for children to socialize but my children would disagree. Playtimes, yes – they made the most of them – but they always wished they could have had longer. They would spend playtime in the company of their friends and many other children continuously and yet they were all being restricted and interrupted by lessons; they did not have enough time to invent games that could last a considerable amount of time.

Towards the end of primary school, playtime became more structured with an element of teacher control: older children were encouraged to look out for the younger children and include them in their games. A class rota appeared where the children were occasionally expected to take their turn in sweeping up and cleaning the dinner hall after lunch, which meant missing valuable playtime. Communication with peers came in all-too-brief bursts as they hurried between lessons or chatted on the bus journey to and from school. There just wasn't enough time for them to do what children want to do: simply talk and play together. This could actually be considered disastrous for any species that learns naturally through curiosity, communication and having the freedom to play and explore at will.

NOTE: Having nurtured my own children through nature and seen how they can thrive when they incorporate the knowledge gained through their play, I consider this vital in the early development of all children.

What made school disappointing for individualized attention is that they were being left in an environment where the children greatly outnumbered the adults around them, effectively rendering the possibility of being nurtured individually zero. There really is no hope of all children feeling naturally nurtured in a school environment.

Children will adapt to school routines, of course, or they will try to. My own children looked forward to break times and they placed their trust in the adults around them. They soon identified the nice adults and the not-so-nice ones; they recognized that one of their teaching assistants became more approachable towards the end of term. Children can take the time to observe their school environment and take on board what they see; they have a strong sense of right and wrong and yet rarely complain. My children would sometimes like to talk about the good or bad behaviour of others; they were also keen to find out how they should respond to any bad (or unhelpful) behaviour they encountered within the school. For example – one member of staff appeared to develop the unhelpful habit of informing the children 'not to tell tales' each time they attempted to raise a concern about the behaviour of another child. My daughter and her friends experienced this: they came across one child deliberately hurting another in the corridor and they rushed to report what was going on, only to be promptly sent away and told 'not to tell tales'. The following morning I mentioned the incident to the school and the class teacher acted quickly. She talked to the children involved and listened to them, acting on their concerns. This teacher also asked the children to report any concerns directly to her in the future.

In a home environment where a child has been nurtured naturally they are already considered to be part of a family group, where their confidence (and, I believe, their maturity) can develop quickly and with little conscious effort, leaving them free to focus on their interests. In a mainstream school environment children have to become part of a new social group, and some children may find themselves having to make an extreme, conscious effort in order to be accepted into this new group. For some children this acceptance or non-acceptance into the school community may remain the focus of their attention throughout their school years.

Being left at school is a daunting prospect for a very young human to face, particularly if they don't feel inclined to leave their own nurturing environment at home. I've often considered that perhaps these children can see no obvious reason to change their routine. However, some children do leave their home environment willingly and are keen to show their parents and teachers how quickly they can conform to their new school routine; they settle in and see school as a very suitable environment. Should we keep assuming that all children do eventually settle in or come to terms with school? I know many children who have 'given in' reluctantly and I was one myself.

Many parents and educational establishments do see socialization in schools as a natural way of children taking their first steps towards independence by making friends and fitting in, and they believe it does a child good to interact and find their own way. I see it differently: I would say that although children need to socialize they also need considerable time by themselves, to be themselves, in order to observe the world around them. I think this is another balance that needs consideration. After they leave the school environment, never again will they have to spend so much of their time confined in the company of so many peers with so few role models to listen to them.

My own observation and subsequent research into learning within family groups has led me to believe that there are other mammals (of higher intelligence than is generally considered) who are similar to us in many ways that already have a much better grasp of how to find a balance of nurturing through nature than we human beings. Elephants raise their calves in an environment where the adults outnumber the young. They appear to nurture a respect for nature that protects these youngsters as they develop. They learn the skills they need to survive and they do this within a large family group. These young mammals are no doubt capable of learning individually, forming their own groups and playing elsewhere, and yet they stay and are encouraged by their elders to bond with group members. The urge to play for youngsters in this group remains strong and they have the freedom to play whenever they feel inclined and it is safe to do so.

Michael Garstang highlights evidence of this type of learning:

Elephants' awareness of others or, at the very least, an acute awareness of their surroundings is illustrated by an incident observed by Jennifer Dieudonne in the Etosha National Park in Namibia in 2010. Dewdrops tracing the intricate geometry of a giant spider web stretched across a game path were glinting in the rays of the rising sun. A herd of elephants was coming down the trail heading straight toward the jeweled web. Just before reaching it, each giant animal, including the younger calves, stepped off the trail and carefully went around the web. (Garstang 2015, p.49)

A thought occurred to me following a documentary I had seen about a group of orphaned elephants. They were playing and interacting with each other and trying to get along as one new social group, with just one or two keepers looking out for them. Their behaviour was distinctively different to that of their peers who were developing under the watchful eye of familiar family members. I compared the playful behaviour of the young elephants in their own family group to the playful behaviour of their orphaned peers, and I found myself further comparing this to children who play at home in their family group and those who have to try to fit in to a new social group of peers in a school environment, a place where they spend considerable amounts of time away from their established family group.

To help further explain my thoughts, I can give a recent example of why the behaviour of these elephants reminded me of human youngsters at play. We went along with our children to a 'home educators' afternoon' at a beautiful country-house setting with magnificent gardens. Schools were also in attendance up until three o'clock; during the afternoon I was able to see my children interacting with other home-educated families and the many groups of school children. The school children would appear together following a teacher or two. They were led from one attraction to another, appearing as an excited gaggle of noise that would then fade into the distance before another group came along. Very little attention appeared to be placed on their environment and even though they looked and sounded excited they remained very focused on those who were walking with them as they were talking to each other most of the time. They would, however, also observe the people passing and some of the children appeared to show off a little more and become louder when groups of other children approached.

The home-educated children appeared quieter, probably just because they were in more diluted groups: some came with their siblings and one parent, others came in family groups; many stayed close to their parents and there were a few off on their own. It was good to hear their occasional laughter and see these children being allowed to run around freely, skipping, doing cartwheels and handstands. Once their peers from school had boarded their buses the remaining children had the venue to themselves to re-visit the many attractions as often as they wished and at their own leisure.

Our own children (like most children) were keen to explore and run: they asked to go to the gardens first where they ran ahead and then back to us; they did this throughout the afternoon until we caught up with them at a stand or attraction. They went back for a second visit to the piglets, and we watched pottery being made and stayed for quite some time at the longbow- and sword-making areas. They saw a family of ducks and one of the staff kindly pointed out to them a nest hidden in the trees belonging to a great spotted woodpecker; we watched closely as apparently there were youngsters being fed regularly.

I found myself naturally comparing the behaviour of the children to that of other young mammals at play and the group of orphaned elephants in particular, as their behaviour while being led by keepers reminded me, very much, of the school children being led by their teaching staff back to their buses. The children remaining and exploring freely with their parents were able to behave similarly to the young elephants developing naturally within a family group.

NOTE: I can't help but think that the more we consider ourselves to be the most intelligent species the more we appear to be moving our children away from what naturally sustains them.

What I have seen throughout my children's development is that children can appreciate and respect the natural world when they have the opportunity to play in it from a young age. I have recognized that children become more aware of their environment and more tolerant and accepting of each other when they don't have the added pressure placed upon them to socialize and fit into a new social group first. As a result of my observations I do not see school as the only suitable place to socialize; it just happens to be the only available option for many. Home educators, including myself, believe that daily life encounters, communicating with family members, joining clubs and meeting other home-educating groups and families certainly suffice.

Modern society still has a long way to go to get the balance of schooling right. Children have an enthusiasm to learn but they do this instinctively through play in their early years. The only place my own children could learn through play uninhibited was in their home environment. We don't interrupt their games and when their friends come over they know they can play, eat and talk when they choose.

If you were to ask my children they would still say that play and friendships had been their only reasons for going to school, and they made the most of their allocated times for play while they were there. So detailed are their accounts of playing at school that I can still picture them in my mind today. I don't recall them talking about lessons in the same way. Both children are game innovators: they talk through and invent the games. As the games came to fruition they found themselves being approached by other year groups hoping to join in. At first, this surprised me as both children were considered to be quieter members of their peer group and as such would not necessarily expect to be approached by others so readily. So I came to the conclusion that their popularity in the playground was because they were confident in their ability to play naturally. They were able to get a good 'chase' game going with lots of children joining in: these games normally involved them being in an animal pack, so they could all mimic the behaviour of other animals. All children have a fascination for the natural world and so are naturally interested in predator-type chase games where they can take on different roles.

Ian often says that if you know what you are talking about you can talk with confidence and others will listen. Play is important to children: it's what they talk about the most and so perhaps we should all take the time to listen.

PLAY

Play – where do I start? – at home, in the garden, with us
or at school, with friends, it's what children do best.

(My own observation)

Whether children play alone or together in their natural environment they develop an awareness of their surroundings and during play they imagine, invent, discover, discuss, create, describe, build, destroy, explore, have fun, get messy, get wet, laugh, cry, feel happy, feel proud, feel embarrassed, feel sad, feel angry, feel frustrated, show sympathy, show empathy, make mistakes, feel disappointment, try again, sulk, ponder, have success, have adventures, have new ideas, develop ideas, suggest ideas, become confident, become more independent, create rules, break rules, change the rules, see the consequences of their actions, decide what to play, agree what to play, feel hurt, get hurt, feel better, feel good, plan ahead... They develop an awareness of each other and how their own actions can cause a reaction and emotion in others as they adapt and respond to situations. Play is a natural process that enhances natural development.

Dinosaur games were important for our son when he was younger. They still are to some extent, but during his early development they formed the basis of many games, in the sand pit and the paddling pool, Lego and chase. As a result our daughter always wanted to be a baby herbivore and so consequently she would end up in peril. Eventually she changed her tactics and decided she would play at being a pack dinosaur and she would join up with her brother. It would then be my turn to be the predator; they would run and hide and I would stalk, ambush or hunt them down while they tried to make it to the safety of 'the gates' (home base).

FRIENDSHIPS

They would also play these games with their friends. Meeting other children with similar interests in their early years and making friends through their interests along the way are what every parent hopes for. We hoped for this ourselves and so we were of course relieved when they developed great friendships.

However, there were still occasions when my young children would say to me, 'Who will I play with?' I would normally respond with, 'Don't worry, you'll be fine, you're good at making friends and you are lovely. Remember to smile and if they smile back you could talk to them.' I have also reminded them that if they do find themselves outside with nobody to play with then to realize they are not alone: there's always a 'little bug guy' to search for or they could watch the birds...or a spider, as watching them make their webs can be mesmerizing.

NOTE: Darwin observed flying spiders on board the ship HMS *Beagle*. They would be blown aboard the ship on a current of air; these spiders use a silky spun web balloon to cross the seas. We haven't seen this for ourselves (as yet) but we have seen many spiders capture and paralyse their lunch, the largest meal being a butterfly.

Being there to give advice and guidance before and after school helps in developing what I call 'social tact': to deal with their feelings and how they should tackle various situations, particularly when it comes to more 'difficult' and outspoken peers or teaching staff.

 NOTE: Playing music at home (or in the car if you have a school run) can change one's mood and can really help with many situations.

The behaviour of some children and/or adults in the school environment can be a concern and it is important that young children have the confidence to handle rude or unpleasant encounters. I can remember my son's response when he first encountered a boy who was behaving in an unkind way; we were in our local park at the time. My son turned to me and said quietly, 'He isn't very nice.' He could see that the boy was being unkind by blocking the slide and I quietly admired my son as he calmly wandered off to play elsewhere. I can remember feeling impressed with his ability to recognize and acknowledge bad behaviour at just three years old. Over the years both children have come to understand that situations and circumstances can sometimes cause children to become unpleasant or appear rude, particularly when adjusting to the school environment.

Our children made friends with siblings from the same families, so they became a mixed group of older and younger siblings who could meet regularly and play together. Because of this, parties and sleepovers or campovers were (and still are) easy to arrange. They soon made other friends in the school environment.

They remain in touch with their friends and their families, and occasionally we take the opportunity to catch up and socialize in a group with adults and children chatting together initially before the children disappear off to play. The children do still home in on us but most of the time these days it's more of a refreshment stop before play resumes again.

The same applies at family events, of course, and because of this we have not seen a need to join a home school group, but there are many groups around for those who do. Our children prefer to socialize with their friends in familiar environments and continue to meet new friends naturally through their clubs, interests and outings.

🐉 **NOTE:** My daughter plays on the 'How to Train Your Dragon' online computer game. This game allows players to 'chat' (by typing what they would like to say) to each other; my daughter is encouraged (by her parents!) to chat only with her local friends as they fly their dragons alongside others worldwide. I sometimes join in with her game, having mastered the art of flying my own dragon. I still find the landings tricky and so I felt pleased recently when my daughter kindly offered to land for me: she took control and landed me on a rocky cliff edge, where I joined lots of other dragons and their riders from around the world. My daughter smiled at me reassuringly and said, 'There you go, Mum – make friends.' I panicked as she flew off and left me to it, spinning my dragon around and accidentally sending a blast of fire directly into the group of dragons. I eventually backed up a little too far and fell off the cliff into the sea.

Feeling self-conscious is typical of me if left alone in a large group, especially if I don't have anything in my hands to hold. I'll do it, but I'm not comfortable. I don't think I'm alone; not all of us are comfortable interacting with strangers (or dragons) in large groups, and that's absolutely fine of course. I, like my children, my husband and many others I know, prefer to make friends over time, and it's not something that can be assumed or demanded. Sometimes a large group can be a very lonely place to be.

Lonely moments for children can be quickly overcome by seeking out the habitats of fascinating and often-minuscule inhabitants of the world: beetles and bugs.

(My own observation)

Chapter Fourteen

PARENTING WISDOM AND SOCIAL TACT

Parenting 'wisdom' is what many of us would regard as parenting 'knowledge'. The term was introduced in our home following a reference to it in a dinosaur cartoon; my children saw how the mother dinosaur passed on her 'wisdoms', as she called them, to her son. My children used to watch this cartoon regularly and so it became a familiar term and one that we still use today.

Subtle social tact is something children learn from their parents and role models. School environments don't always have the time to teach social manners and so I think it is of utmost importance that children develop these early on. We can naturally help them to develop this by simply ensuring that our own 'social tact' is evident and obvious at all times, and particularly when our children are present.

COMMUNICATION

Most mothers with younger children will naturally adopt a soft tone of voice and a kind manner; I did this with my own children and discovered that it remained useful throughout their development. I found that if I communicated with them in a kind manner and gave them the time to talk to me then I would always get a mature response back.

NOTE: In fact all I'm doing is giving them the same level of respect that I would if I was talking to an adult.

A soft tone of voice is also a good starting point when teaching children social tact and manners. Many parents assume that developing independence and confidence are important when it comes to a child being able to interact and communicate effectively, and for some this may be the case; but I have found that a quiet maturity and a polite manner will gain respect from peers and adults. Knowing when, how and who to approach is a required life skill. No adult should expect to be centre stage in a conversation, just as no child should expect to be ignored. A delicate balance between all parties is required, and we have found that subtle guidance within the family group has ensured good social tact.

A mindful parent will be able to read how comfortable their child feels in any given environment just by looking for the emotion shown in their eyes. We can't always tell if a child is listening and so we often find ourselves relying on eye contact when parenting. Most parents use eye contact and body language without even realizing they are doing so.

Children like to talk freely and to interact with society and family members of all ages. I have found that there is a delicate balance to be established when it comes to developing their confidence and maturity, and they do this naturally by observing adults: they talk to them, listen to them and respond to them. Children can have a lot to say and so with this in mind it's important that they develop this natural sense of understanding and politeness, and know when (or when not) to join in socially.

As a parent I feel saddened when I see young children being impolitely snapped at by their teachers, other adults or other children in the school environment. If an adult needs reprimanding for something, they are reminded in a way that does not offend or upset; they are shown a level of respect. Children (no matter how often they've been reminded already) deserve to be treated with that same level of respect. I have often heard and seen groups of children being ordered around in the school environment and thought that it's not something that would be tolerated in the workplace by adults.

NOTE: I will ask my children why they think a particular person behaves the way they do (good or bad) and I inevitably agree with their observations. From an early age children develop an understanding of the behaviour of others and learn from the consequences of those behaviours.

BEDTIME

I enjoyed settling my children down to sleep, particularly once we had established a good routine. A little bit of patience and stamina was required along the way...especially when they were newborns. Either my husband or I would hold them as they went to sleep but once they were a little older we would rock them gently in their seat or cradle. When they were of an age where they could sit up I developed a bedtime routine, and it was one that worked for us all. It would start following their evening drink of milk and bedtime story, and continue as follows.

- En route to bed there would be lots of cuddles with instinctive sniffs and kisses to the top of the head before doing the final nappy change and laying down next to them on the bed (any bed, and ensuring they couldn't roll off of course).

- The next step would be to ensure our faces were level and turned towards each other. I would then start to do a series of slow blinks. Quite often at this point a little hand would reach over to my face and I would take hold of it gently and lower it back down into that familiar sleeping position that babies adopt, ensuring that I kept slowly blinking.

- They would start to do the same long blinks and in no time at all they would fall asleep. I would observe them for a little while longer just to ensure they had fallen fast asleep.

- Then it was just a case of gently lifting them, holding them really close and carrying them to their room and cot, being sure to hold their head and stroke it if they stirred as I slowly lowered them. I remember the cot sides having to be clicked into place, and this would sometimes startle them and their arms would jump, but they didn't wake.

This worked for both of them and a habit formed: the process developed and over time they would naturally fall asleep with hardly any blinks needed at all. Before long all I needed to do was to stand over their cot and stroke their forehead as this always appeared to calm them; I would also do a series of soft 'shhh' sounds as I left the room because I believe remaining calm and quiet is crucial at bedtimes. I never felt tempted to rush back in if they stirred: this could quickly have developed into a habit and perhaps even startle or upset them. I would sometimes feel that I needed to wait outside their room in case that extra bit of gentle reassurance was required and, if so, would creep back in before they had the chance to fully wake up. A gentle stroke to the forehead would always suffice.

It's also worth noting the timing of a young child's afternoon nap, the emphasis being on 'afternoon' and not early evening. We discovered they would go to sleep on time each evening but only if they didn't sleep after four o'clock in the afternoon. If a child falls asleep (or stays asleep) after that time then the chances are they may not be tired when expected, and good sleeping routines are essential for a child. With this in mind, trips out in the car are best structured around this. We aimed (quite successfully) to be home by late afternoon when we had young children in order to maintain their good bedtime routines, and recognizing this natural need enabled us to ensure it was met.

BUILDING THE BONDS OF FRIENDSHIP

Our children have always been encouraged to play together in their natural surroundings and this enabled them to build on those important bonds. They have been raised together with no expectations whatsoever about what they might choose to play with. We did not attach any significance to their gender, as they are both children and as such they could explore and play with their toys or anything else that happened to be around. DVD cases, for example, were often lined up to become an enclosure for a pack or herd of animals.

When they were settled and secure in their surroundings we invited friends into the home environment. Having already established a really strong bond with each other and to nature, they continued to develop bonds, this time with their friends. Initially (when they were younger) this could be achieved without peer pressure or technology becoming a distraction. They happily shared their home, their garden and their belongings as they communicated and played together in a group.

Currently, now they are older, whether it's face to face or communicating via technology they still share friends and appreciate each other's likes and dislikes. They all have different interests and will sit down to eat together and talk generally, just as the adults around them do. Having said that, on one occasion when a friend first came round she stood up mid-meal and declared 'boys are all pigs'. Her brother protested a little but he, along with the others, found it funny.

Children require constant but subtle social advice and guidance as they grow; they look for inspiration and attention from their parents. Peers can influence them and this could be good or bad, and so it seems sensible that good routines and communication are established early to enable children to learn what's wise from their own family group, just as other mammals do.

MEALTIMES

Children can be as fussy or as accommodating as adults when it comes to food. We simply developed a routine and introduced the healthy food before any 'treats'. Water, milk and watered-down fresh fruit drinks were our children's preferred options and these were also introduced before anything else; they haven't yet developed a taste for cordial or fizzy drinks. I always ensured that when a new food type was being introduced the meal was served with at least one familiar item which I knew they liked on their plate, alongside the new. This avoided disappointment whenever they sat down to eat, perhaps making them feel more inclined to give the new food a try.

TANTRUMS

Ian and I agreed from the start that we would have a zero-tolerance approach to tantrums should they arise. Both children have always known this to be the case: if they throw a tantrum we go home. As a result we only ever had to carry out our warning to each of them once. They discovered that we always meant what we said; they naturally accepted this and respected our decisions, particularly as we always took the time to explain them. Important tip: stay calm. The louder they get, the quieter you should get, but above all remain concise: they can't be led to believe that they can sway your mind by behaving badly.

ROLE MODELS

Parents who consider themselves easily bored could naturally assume that their children require constant distractions and so provide them with entertainment. Parents who expect to be entertained could also assume that their children need to be entertained, and act accordingly. If parents shout demands at their children they may (or may not) be surprised when their children shout back. If a parent shows they have superstitions, their children may also become superstitious. So sometimes as role models we need to consider that our good intentions could in fact be detrimental, particularly when we consider that children (and adults) can quickly adopt the behaviours of anyone they perceive to be a role model.

WHEN IT'S TIME TO GO HOME

On days out or when we found ourselves ready to leave a venue such as an adventure park it would occasionally be obvious to my husband and me that our children were still absorbed in their environment. Rather than informing them that it was time to go, Ian and I would give them at least five or ten minutes' notice. When they were younger we ensured we always gave them something worthwhile to leave for, so it was more a case of 'If we leave now then you'll have time to set up camp and watch the bats' (for example).

 NOTE: Discovering that we could move them along naturally by offering nature enticements was extremely useful and beneficial.

NURTURE

According to my dictionary the definition of 'nurture' is to train, educate, bring up and nourish. I would add one vital ingredient – 'respect' – as I believe children naturally develop an understanding of respect when we take the time to nurture them. Ian and I enjoy nurturing our children in their home environment and in their natural world. We enjoy enticing their laughter, reducing their tears, holding their hands, ruffling their hair, hugging them better, settling them to sleep, lifting them up into and down out of trees, encouraging them to be polite, to play nicely and to share, acknowledging their presence (and that of wildlife), laughing with them (and not at them), and encouraging their interests and their friendships along the way.

HAPPINESS

I'm often asked by my children, 'Imagine if you had an endless supply of wishes – what would you wish for first?' They will also repeatedly ask, for example, what my favourite animal is. These are questions that most children ask. How do I know this? I used to ask my parents the same questions. They normally pop up in conversation when a child feels excited or happy, just out of curiosity, and it can often be the trigger for a happy conversation when the person responds. My own well being and happiness naturally improves when I share my children's enthusiasm for being curious. I feel that this type of repetition and recounting is very important in their learning: they will read the same book a number of times, and recount particular events many times. They also enjoy hearing about how Ian and I used to think and play as children; they build a picture by asking us what we like. Sometimes they say they can't imagine us when we were young and try to find out how we might have felt at the time; we talk and we reminisce whenever the moment naturally occurs.

NOTE: Talk of happiness reminded me that my children recently came across the 'happy face spider', *Theridion grallator*, while researching online. This became a trigger for them to start comparing other contenders that could be considered 'the most interesting spider'. My son's favourite, the 'slingshot spider', was next to be put forward. Having listened to their detailed accounts of both spiders I came to my conclusion: just hearing about the happy face spider made me want to see it, and as for the slingshot spider, one that actually makes a slingshot in order to catch mosquitoes...simply amazing. Both spiders won my vote, exactly as the children predicted!

As we reach the end of this chapter it seems fitting to round it off with a final reminder of the knowledge they can gain through learning this way.

Douglas keeps on eating our strawberries. He climbs into the strawberry patch and eats them. The seeds are in his poo.

(My daughter's observation)
This comment was noted in her journal
during the month of June 2015.

My daughter reported this observation to me. I was then able to encourage her to research (and discuss) the process of seed dispersal where brightly coloured and succulent fruit (with seeds that have indigestible coats) are swallowed by the animal. The seeds then pass through the animal undamaged and are dispersed some distance from the mother plant. This is a natural process ensuring new growth and avoiding overcrowding.

A year at home seems to go much faster than a year in school.

(My son's observation)

Chapter Fifteen

TIME FLIES

If it weren't for my two children and their antics I wouldn't have spent the last eleven fascinating years observing their play. They have inspired me to see for myself the wonders of the world and the universe. I didn't even know how far away the sun was until they came along, but I do know now. I 'get' evolution but still struggle with the mysteries of quantum entanglement, but with Ian still keen to enlighten us it triggers long discussions and interesting family debates.

Dinosaurs were hugely successful and ruled the earth for 165 million years; they were only wiped out because of an unfortunate event. I don't know what the future holds for us but I have come to understand the struggles we will face as a species in the future in order to survive in an overpopulated environment, and how important it is to focus on the next generation and share our concerns with them about our wonderful planet. They need to be mindful, imaginative and creative in order to find survival solutions for all its inhabitants in the years ahead.

When my husband and I took the helm of this 'education' boat and steered our family out into the big wide world, it was obvious from the start that the children had the map, and this has made the journey far more interesting. Children are able to choose where they want to go and as the helmsman you simply get to steer, guide and comment on the journey as you lap up the smooth sailing; you can also advise them to 'hold on' if things get a little choppy. If others become curious enough to bob up alongside your boat and say 'Ahoy there' you can decide whether to share your itinerary with them or just politely sail away, sail off into the sunset perhaps. Looking towards the horizon I can see we have teenage years full steam ahead and I'm also pondering as my son's just asked me if he can have a leopard gecko...which means it's likely my daughter will now ask for a sloth. All aboard then!

The early worm keeps his head down.

(An accidental quote by Ian, my husband)

He meant to say 'The early bird gets the worm' but we rather like this version.

Chapter Sixteen

CHARACTER BUILDING

Everyone at some point has a load to bear and my own children are no exception.

For our son, it's how society sees a dyslexic mind. His calm nature enables him to strive quietly for his dream of becoming a palaeontologist and he certainly has the enthusiasm and determination to achieve this. He has retained the knowledge gained through his early interest and this continues to grow. He likes how his brain works and knows how to use it, and he continues to create physically what he sees visually, so he is doing what dyslexics do best! I would like to have his knowledge and see the prehistoric world how his mind does. It sounds an amazing place.

For our daughter, it was being diagnosed with a rare form of arthritis at the age of three. She has been under the care of our local hospital, another one further afield and also Great Ormond Street Children's Hospital in London since that time; these three small but remarkable teams of health professionals continue to provide her exemplary care as they monitor her condition. It has been a challenging journey for her and she still endures daily injections and medication administered here at home. Her amazing maturity, determination and enthusiasm enable her to lead a normal life; her patience and courage continue to astound us. These days, when she plays her cello, Iris...well, it's a beautiful thing.

It has not gone unnoticed by us that our daughter went into medication-induced remission the same month that she started home education – she is currently arthritis-free. Coincidental maybe, but we have certainly noticed that both of our children are less anxious and more relaxed since leaving school; their confidence is growing daily and they both know we are very proud of them.

My children have discovered many fascinating facts as a result of having their natural curiosity recognized. Whether self-educated, school educated or home educated it is the responsibility of a parent to ensure their child grows up with a respect for nature, an enthusiasm for life, an interest in research and the joy of understanding.

Our children's world has been shaped by their boundless curiosity, their bond to nature and to each other, their environment, their circumstances and of course their genetics, but ultimately it's how we nurture them that could perhaps have the biggest impact on their lives.

Years from now I hope that our children will look back and think...

There is no school equal to a decent home and
no teacher equal to a virtuous parent.

Mahatma Gandhi (1947)

REFERENCES

Anthony, L. and Spence, G. (2010) *The Elephant Whisperer*. London: Pan Macmillan.

Attenborough, D. (2009) *Life Stories*. London: HarperCollins.

Byers, J.A. (2013) *Animal Behaviour*. London: Oneworld Publications.

Cowell, C. (2014) *The Incomplete Book of Dragons*. London: Hodder Children's Books.

Darwin, C. (2003 [1887]) *The Autobiography of Charles Darwin*. Cambridge: Icon Books.

Durrell, G. (2012) *Encounters with Animals*. London: Penguin Books.

Einstein, A. (2000 [1955]) *The Expanded Quotable Einstein*, edited by A. Calaprice. Princeton, NJ: Princeton University Press.

Garstang, M. (2015) *Elephant Sense and Sensibility: Behavior and Cognition*. London: Academic Press.

Gandhi, M. (2008 [1947]) *India of My Dreams*. Delhi: Rajpal & Sons.

HRH The Prince of Wales, with Juniper, T. and Skelly, I. (2010) *Harmony: A New Way of Looking at Our World*. London: Blue Door, HarperCollins Publishers.

Jekyll, G. (2009 [1899]) *The Beauties of a Cottage Garden*. London: Penguin Books.

Kahn, P.H., Jr and Kellert, S.R. (eds) (2002) *Children and Nature: Psychological, Sociocultural, and Evolutionary Investigations*. Cambridge, MA: MIT Press.

Roberts, M. (1997) *The Man Who Listens to Horses*. London: Arrow Books.

Thomas, A. and Pattison, H. (2009) *How Children Learn at Home*. London: Continuum International Publishing Group.

INDEX